ZAK MORADI

FROM KURDISTAN TO CROKE PARK

MORADI

LIFE BEGINS IN LEITRIM

WITH NIALL KELLY

GILL BOOKS

Gill Books
Hume Avenue
Park West
Dublin 12
www.gillbooks.ie

Gill Books is an imprint of M.H. Gill and Co.

9780717194667

Designed by Typo•glyphix, Burton-on-Trent DE14 3HE
Edited by Jane Rogers
Proofread by Ciara McNee

Printed by CPI Group (UK) Ltd, Croydon, CRO 4YY
This book is typeset in 12.5pt on 18pt Minion Pro.

*The paper used in this book comes from the wood pulp of
sustainably managed forests.*

A CIP catalogue record for this book is available from the
British Library.

5 4 3 2 1

Samme,
Hope you enjoy the
book.
Dad

Dec 22

For Safar, my dad

CONTENTS

CONTENTS

PROLOGUE

You already know me.

Maybe you've already heard me tell some of my story: the Kurdish lad who was born in an Iraqi refugee camp during the Saddam Hussein dictatorship and who ended up hurling for Leitrim.

There are thousands of others just like me. We're your neighbours. We're your colleagues. We're your classmates, your team-mates, your friends. We're engineers and plumbers and software developers and painters and everything in between.

We're the lad who owns the restaurant down the road – you know the one, the place that does the best kebabs in town – and we're the doctor who keeps telling you not to eat too many of them.

We're the nippy fella in at corner-forward who is going to wreck your head for the whole afternoon because he's simply not going to stop running. And we're the lad who is back out there the very next morning, setting out the cones and the drills for the under-13s training session.

You see, you already know me.

I'm living proof of the céad míle fáilte. Because Ireland might not be the country of my birth, but it's the country I love. Thousands like me came here with nothing, with no place to call home, hopeful that some country would accept us. And Ireland was the one. Ireland welcomed us with open arms. Ireland gave us every opportunity. We went to college here, got degrees here, got great jobs here. The community took us in as their own. We learned the history and the culture, joined the clubs, played the games. We started families here. We made a life. Ireland gave us something special, the greatest gift of all, and inside our hearts there is great love for Ireland.

I told you, you already know me.

I am Zemnako Moradi, but you can call me Zak. I am a refugee. I am Kurdish. I am Irish.

This is my story.

BORN INTO WAR

I was born on 16 January 1991. The bombing started the very next day.

I wasn't born in a hospital. I never had a birth cert. I was born in a refugee camp on the outskirts of the city of Ramadi in Iraq, in a little house made of mud. It wasn't our home – it could never be – but it was all we had.

Ten years earlier, the Iran–Iraq war had forced my parents, my brothers, my sister, their relatives and their friends out of their homes and into this strange place where they didn't belong and they weren't welcome: Al-Tash camp, a refugee camp set up by the Iraqi government but a prison camp in all but name, where they were hemmed in by barbed-wire fences and strictly forbidden to leave.

War had already taken everything my family had. All they had left was the hope that this wouldn't last for ever, and that some day they could go home.

And now war – the Gulf War – had found them again.

When Saddam Hussein ordered his Iraqi army troops to invade Kuwait in the summer of 1990, America and its allies intervened. For thirty-eight days and thirty-eight nights in early 1991, the sound of bombs filled the air. They fell near us and they fell far away, on army bases and bridges and roads, crippling Iraq. They called it Operation Desert Storm.

Inside the refugee camp, the people sensed the danger that was coming in the weeks before those first attacks. Terrified, some families started to dig, realising that even a shallow underground bunker might give them some shelter and a better chance of survival than nothing at all. Others found whatever bits of wood they could and nailed them across the windows of their house. They didn't do it to protect the glass; they did it to protect themselves. The fear of an attack using chemical weapons was never far from their minds.

But when the bombs landed nearby, they ran outside, panicked, not knowing where they might find shelter. The ground shook beneath their feet. The doors rattled on their hinges. The walls of their houses felt like they were wobbling where they stood. They ran, preferring to take their chances outside rather than run the risk of their house coming down on top of them.

An Iraqi army plane was shot out of the sky over their heads. They listened for each new explosion, desperately trying to place where it was, fearing that the rockets that were coming closer and closer would finally come for them. They didn't even know if they would still be alive when that day came, or which was more likely to kill them: the bombs or the starvation.

Of all of the tough times that my family had to endure over the years, my mam, Gohar, often looks back at this time as the most brutal, the worst of the worst. She and my dad, Safar, had eight hungry children to feed, and now a new-born ninth in their arms, and in the midst of war, food was the rarest commodity of all. The laws of supply and demand have no pity or mercy, and whatever little food was available became extortionately expensive, even to those who did have money.

Because, to put it simply, there was none. The bombs wiped out almost an entire country's worth of power plants and oil refineries. With very little electricity or fuel, it was nearly impossible to produce food, and even harder to distribute what little there was. To make matters worse, the economic sanctions placed on Iraq by America and its allies effectively paralysed any attempts to import food into the country.

Our family's tractor was the only thing that saved us from an even more dire situation in those weeks. Somehow, my parents were able to get their hands on some wheat, and mill it using the tractor, giving my mam flour to make enough naan bread to keep us all from going hungry.

One of my dad's uncles said that I would grow up to be tough because I had been born among bombs, born into war. That I would be clever. That I would hate any sort of fighting and rows and arguments.

In later years, when the war in Iraq had stopped for a time and the world's eyes had moved on to another conflict in a different place, the Secretary-General of the United Nations became a familiar face on our television as he pleaded for peace. My family saw a resemblance in me: I was also a diplomat, a peacemaker. They nicknamed me Kofi Annan.

On 23 February 1991, the bombing finally stopped. A few days later, the Gulf War was over.

I was five weeks old.

THE KURDS

D on't bother looking for Kurdistan on any map. You won't find it. You'll find Iraq and Iran, Turkey and Syria, but no Kurdistan.

Our homeland, which stretches across the Middle East and Western Asia, has existed in one form or another for almost a thousand years, but now it's invisible. When Britain and France and their allies sat down to carve up the Ottoman Empire in the aftermath of the First World War, we were the people who were forgotten. A hundred years later, we're still suffering the consequences.

That is our history, a history of broken promises and betrayal. This is why we say that the Kurds have no friends but the mountains. We know where we stand. The mountains are the only ones who will help us, protect us and defend us. They are the only ones who will never abandon us.

It's hard to even accurately count how many Kurds there are now because our history is a history of separation too, of heart-breaking goodbyes and families who didn't know if they would ever see their loved ones again. Without a recognised home to call our own, we have been scattered to the four corners of the globe. There are close to forty million of us, if not more. Whatever the exact number, the Kurds remain the largest ethnic group anywhere in the world without their own country.

It shouldn't have been this way. The first attempt to redraw the Middle East after the First World War, the 1920 Treaty of Sèvres, included provisions for an independent Kurdistan. But that treaty was never ratified, and when the Treaty of Lausanne was agreed in its place in 1923, there wasn't a single mention of Kurdistan or the Kurds. It was as if we had never existed.

Instead, our homeland was split into four different regions, each belonging to a different country, and it remains that way to this day. Each region has its own name, named in Kurdish after the four points of the compass: Bakur to the north, which is in Turkey; Başûr to the south, which is in Iraq; Rojhelat to the east, which is in Iran; and Rojava to the west, which is in Syria.

Millions of Kurds live in each of these regions, but we will always be a minority wherever we are. The parts of our Kurdish identity that are most important to us – our language, our culture, our traditions – are feared and regarded with suspicion by the states we have been forced to live in. Our flag, a red, white and green tricolour with the Kurdish sun in the middle, is seen as provocative. Even our language is seen as a threat; but there's a Kurdish saying that if our mother tongue shakes your nation, you've built your nation on our land.

For the last hundred years, we have been persecuted for who we are, for wanting to be ourselves. There have been brutal massacres and unspeakable atrocities, tens of thousands of men, women and children murdered for the crime of being Kurdish. We have suffered genocide. Entire villages have been wiped out in horrific chemical attacks.

You may not be aware of this history, you may never have heard of these atrocities, and I wouldn't be surprised. It happened to the Kurds. Nobody talks about the Kurds.

HOME

I magine what it's like to lose everything. My parents did.

Before I was born, and before all the trouble began, they lived a quiet life on the outskirts of the mountain city of Sarpel Zahaw, which is in Rojhelat, the Kurdistan of Iran, only a few pucks of a ball from the border with the Kurdistan of Iraq.

Qadri, the rural part of Zahaw that my family comes from, isn't all that different from your typical village in Ireland. It's a small, tight-knit community where everybody knows everybody else. It has been home to the same few extended families down through the generations, and you generally don't have to go too far before you bump into someone you are related to, whether by blood or by marriage. My parents were surrounded by family there. My dad was one of seven children and his dad, my grandfather, was a wealthy man with plenty of land to share out between them as they got married and started families of their own.

This was home: green fields nestled in among the Zagros Mountains, set against a postcard backdrop of peaks and valleys in the near distance. My dad's side of the family have always been farmers: vegetables mainly, maybe some tomatoes alongside the cucumbers, with some sheep and goats as well, and, in recent years, a few beehives for good measure.

For most of my uncles, farming was life, but my dad was always more interested in pursuing an education, with a little bit of farming on the side. While his brothers sowed and harvested, he would travel into Zahaw city, where my grandparents owned a shop and a beautiful three-storey house with seven bedrooms, and he would study Farsi there. In later years, I realised that he could write in three languages, Kurdish, Farsi and Arabic.

Life in Zahaw was simple and it was peaceful. My parents had their own two-storey house, and their own car – at that time a luxury that very few people could afford. They had their family nearby, and that was everything that they could have wanted for a happy life.

But for Kurds in Iran in the 1970s, life could never be truly happy because they were missing the one thing that mattered to them above all else: their freedom. Under the Shah – the King of Iran, Mohammad Reza Pahlavi – they were treated as second-class citizens.

The Shah celebrated Iran's Persian past, and looked to build a Persian future, but this was a multicultural place full of many different people who already had their own identities, customs and traditions. They didn't want to be Persian. They were proud of who they were.

Kurdish people had their land taken away from them. Kurdish leaders were executed. Even for the richest of the rich among the Kurdish community, for the people who seemingly had everything, life was tough because they couldn't be fully themselves.

And then, in 1979, revolution came to Iran. War was not far behind it.

WE NEED TO GO NOW

Let me teach you a few words of Kurdish:

'Slaw, choni?'	('Hello, how are you?')
'Min bashim, supas'	('I am fine, thank you')
'Eme le metirsidayin, pewiste esta birroyin'	
	('We are in danger, we need to go now')

The late 1970s was a time of unprecedented change and turmoil in Iran. People were taking to the streets to demand change. Opposition and protests became more and more widespread and turned into revolution. In 1979, fearing for his safety, the Shah fled the country and went into exile. After having ruled for nearly forty years, he lost his power and lost control of the country. Without him the monarchy quickly collapsed, and Iran was transformed into an Islamic republic led by its Supreme Leader, Ayatollah Khomeini.

After the revolution, the dust gradually settled, but for the people the uncertainty continued. Tensions grew between Iran and Iraq. The Ayatollah hoped that his Islamic Revolution might extend across the border, but Saddam Hussein, the president of Iraq, viewed this new Iranian republic as a clear and present threat to Iraqi safety. In the cities and villages across Iran, nobody knew whether to expect war or peace.

Then, on 22 September 1980, Iraq launched its first air strikes on Iranian territory. That was the beginning of the Iran–Iraq war, which would last almost eight years until the summer of 1988, with hundreds of thousands dead on both sides.

As the Iraqi troops crossed the border and closed in on Zahaw, some people fled east towards Tehran, believing that a big city could offer them some protection. Others looked to the mountains – that was where they felt they could be safe. Others headed for the border, hoping to find shelter in Iraq.

My parents were forced to flee Zahaw in October 1980. They grabbed whatever they could, packed it into their tractor and trailer alongside my three eldest brothers, Raoof, Osman and Mokhtar, and my eldest sister, Ghazal, and they ran. The sleepy little farming village in the mountains wasn't their home any more. Now it was an Iraqi army post.

Overnight, my family lost pretty much everything they had. In that first week they moved from village to village, frantically trying to figure out a path to safety. They first went to Qadri Jayran, a nearby village, where they stayed for two nights before moving on to a village called Serqela, and then on again to Taperash.

Every stop was a brief one, a moment to weigh up the danger and decide on their next move. After three nights in Taperash, they left again and, too frightened to stay in Iran any longer, set off into the mountains with the aim of crossing the border into the Kurdistan of Iraq.

As soon as they were safely across, they found a place to settle called Haji Lar and parked their tractor. It was barely a mile or two from the border, but that was where they wanted to be. They still held on to the hope that this might just be temporary. But even if that was true, even if they could have gone back, everything was gone, either flattened by war or robbed from the rubble that was left behind. They had lost everything. They might not have known it that first night as they tried to get some sleep, but this new and unfamiliar place was now the closest thing they had to a home. They would stay in Haji Lar for the next ten months.

At first they lived in a mud house, built by hand entirely out of bricks made of dried clay. It wasn't much, but it did give them shelter, a little bit of privacy and protection. Two or three months later, as the winter months set in and the number of refugees climbed higher and higher, the Iraqi authorities tried to take some steps to address the crisis. The government allocated my family a house in Haji Lar. They lived there until the summer of 1981.

In the chaos of war that had swallowed up their village, the family had split up. While my parents and brothers and sister settled in Haji Lar, if only temporarily, my grandmother and some of her brothers had headed north to a town called Sirwan, where the only shelter they and their fellow refugees could find was in a little camp of tents.

They heard the sound of engines flying overhead, but they never expected that they would be the targets. An army plane bombed the tents they were living in. A piece of flying shrapnel struck my grandmother's brother in the face; another hit my grandmother in the arm, leaving her with injuries that she never fully recovered from. She needed a sling to support her paralysed arm for the rest of her life, a permanent reminder of the day the rockets struck.

THE JOURNEY

The war raged on. My family had been living in Haji Lar for ten months when the Iraqi government sent the trucks for them. Whatever little sense of control they had managed to regain over their lives while settled there, whatever rhythm and routine their days had found, it was upended again without warning. There could have been close to two hundred Kurdish refugee families living there when the trucks rolled in, herded them up like chickens or goats, and moved them off to another new place that they knew absolutely nothing about.

The new place was called Belula, it turned out, but that hardly mattered because five weeks later they were moved again. The Iraqi government wasn't overly concerned about comfort or compassion. The authorities were, however, concerned about having large groups of Iranian Kurds living in their country – and living so close to the border –

while the two countries were at war. Any one of these Kurds could be a spy, or fighting for Iran. If they put all the Kurdish refugees together in one area, they only had one place to worry about.

When they were all moved on from Belula after a few weeks, they were taken to the middle of nowhere. The area was called Sangar but that was its only real identifying feature. Otherwise, it was just remote rural scrubland, with a few trees and fields, on the banks of the Sirwan River, in the Kurdistan of Iraq. This was the spot the Iraqi government had chosen to gather Kurdish families together, turning the empty land into a mini refugee camp of sorts. It was an awful place, more suited to lizards and snakes than to humans, as my family soon found out.

For close to nine months, they were expected to live with no home other than the two tents given to them by the government and no food other than the basic rations that they were provided with every week. For my mam, life was even tougher. She was pregnant while they were kept in these awful conditions in Sangar, and that is where my brother was born. They named him Bakhtiar.

The next time the trucks came, it felt like there were hundreds of them. The army loaded everybody up and started the long drive south into the middle of the country, far away from the border, until they pulled up in another barren wasteland on the outskirts of the city of Ramadi. The place barely existed, but it would become known as Al-Tash camp. It was 15 July 1982, and this would be my family's home for the vast majority of the next twenty years.

To describe Al-Tash camp as it was when my parents first arrived is easy; there was nothing to describe. It was dead, a virtual no man's land. The summer sun was unbearable, baking the barren ground even harder. There were no buildings, no trees to protect them from the elements, so when the wind whipped in, everything was covered in a blanket of dust. Once again, they were forced to live in tents, and one of their main concerns was how to stop them from blowing away, and how to get them back again when they inevitably did. There was no water to drink, and no obvious way to access it; but for the food parcels, there wouldn't have been anything to eat either.

We still have an old black notebook at home, battered by the years, its hard cover now coming loose from its stitching at the front: my dad's diary. It's written in a mix of Kurdish, Arabic and Farsi that I can't really understand, but in it are some of his memories of life in Al-Tash camp:

There were around 12,000 families there at the time. People were suffering and not treated well. The basic human needs were not provided to the people. It was a very tough time there. There was no life, we were basically in a desert and people were building their own houses with no structure. It was highly overpopulated and no one was allowed out of the camp at all. It felt very suffocating and controlled. There was even barbed wire surrounding the camp to prevent anyone leaving.

Diary of Safar Moradi, Al-Tash refugee camp

In those early years, the refugees were strictly forbidden to leave the camp area. The perimeter was surrounded by barbed-wire fences, the jagged edges of the steel deterring anybody who would even consider it. This was no place for help or humanitarian aid. This was effectively a prison, but people were terrified that it might be something worse. Nobody was foolish enough to presume that they were safe here. Whenever they were moved to a new place, they feared that it might be the last place, that this would be the place they had been brought to die. Where they had been brought to be killed.

The refugees lived in the tents for most of their first year in Al-Tash. It slowly became clear that the Iraqi government hadn't brought them here to murder them, but they weren't particularly interested in helping them either. Whatever life they were going to make, they would have to make for themselves.

WE'RE NOT FROM HERE

For as long as I can remember, I knew that Al-Tash camp was not our home. I was a child. I was too young to know that our life was not a normal life, or to even begin to imagine what any other kind of life there might be, but I understood that nobody wanted to stay in this place for ever. Everybody was trying to get away from here. Everybody was trying to get back to somewhere else.

And I knew that place was Kurdistan. I knew that was where we belonged. I knew that we were Kurds.

Most people in Iraq spoke Arabic, but everybody I knew spoke Kurdish. The schools in the camp had all been set up by the United Nations and the Iraqi government, and all the classes were taught through Kurdish. You only needed Arabic if you went to secondary school. There were no secondary schools in the camp – the nearest ones were in Ramadi, and classes there were taught through Arabic. A lot of Kurdish children didn't go to those schools for that simple reason. The only Arabic words they knew were the ones they had picked up from the TV or from watching dubbed movies, and if they didn't speak the language, it would only be a matter of time before they were expelled. They left school at twelve or thirteen instead.

My parents, like a lot of parents, hoped that we wouldn't be living there long enough to ever need Arabic. It was more important that we learned Farsi, which would be a lot more practical when the time eventually came for us to move back to the Kurdistan of Iran.

Officially, the school day was a short one. We were only there for two or three hours in the morning. Some teachers set up private schools in the camp where, for a few dinar, they would teach children Farsi, and that was where we spent most afternoons.

Going home to the Kurdistan of Iran was the dream, but by the time I was born in 1991, a lot of the Kurdish refugees in Al-Tash camp had started to accept their current reality. If they had no choice except to stay in this awful place for now, they would do whatever they could to build a new life out of the dust and the dirt while they were there. As family after family built houses for themselves, the desert wilderness was transformed into a little village with a heartbeat of its own. There were different neighbourhoods dotted throughout the camp, each belonging to different family groups. Just like in Zahaw, we lived with the Qadris, the clan or tribe of my dad's side of the family, and all our nearest neighbours were related to him: uncles and aunts and distant cousins.

We lived in a single-storey mud house with three decent-sized rooms – they had to be big enough for all of us when my two younger brothers were born and our family of thirteen was complete: my mam and dad, Gohar and Safar, my sisters, Ghazal and Halala, my eight brothers, Raoof, Osman, Mokhtar, Bakhtiar, Hoshar, Jamal, Makwan and Reebin, and me. Our house was simple, as all the houses in the camp were. We had a metal tandoor oven that my mam used to make our naan bread, and a little television. We had a bit of garden in the front and in the back, and that was it.

Even at the best of times, the basics were in short supply. Once a week, we would go to visit one of my dad's distant cousins, a man named Hussein. Hussein was a Qadri as well, probably in his seventies, and a person who everybody knew and respected. It was his job to manage the food ration for our community for the week, to make sure that nobody went hungry and that every family got their fair share and no more. The food packages were delivered to Hussein's house and we would go, along with all of the other

31

Qadri families, to discover what we had been allocated for the week ahead: a bag or two of rice, a bag or two of flour, and whatever else was available.

Water was scarce too. In the middle of a desert, there wasn't even much point in looking to the sky and praying for rain. It was years before the UN and the Iraqi government built a pipeline to try to bring a water supply into the camp, and even after that, it was still pure chance if there was anything in the pipes when we went to turn the tap on. Once a month, we might get lucky with a trickle of water, but other than that, we were wasting our time.

Long before that, my older brothers had dug a little well in our back garden, and most other families did the same. It must have taken them a few weeks of digging with their shovels through bone-dry earth until they finally got down far enough into the ground to hit water, but once they had dug it, it was ours, and far more reliable than the pipeline. We attached a rope to the handle of a bucket and lowered it down inside the well until it filled. Sometimes the bucket was too light and it would sit there on the surface, bobbing about annoyingly without filling. I was taught a trick for whenever that happened: we put a stone into the bucket to add an extra little bit of weight before lowering it, and then gravity did the rest of the work for us.

Some days, we would have electricity for three hours; other days, we might have it for ten. The only reason that we had any electricity at all was because someone in the camp had bought a generator and run a line to hook it up to a row or two of houses. The deal was that each house was only allowed to turn on one light in the evening so that there was enough electricity to share out among everyone who had paid to be connected, but a lot of families were happy to sit in the dark or keep the TV switched off for the evening, especially in the summer. If they were only allowed to turn one thing on, it was much more important to use the electricity for their air cooler.

For a lot of the year, we slept outside in the garden – not because we didn't have enough space to sleep indoors, but because it was too warm. At the height of the summer, the temperatures during the day would easily hit the mid-forties Celsius, pushing fifty degrees, and the air cooler became the most important thing any of us owned. Every two hours, one of us had the job of going out to the well, getting a bucket of water, and filling the cooler so that we weren't suffocated in our own homes by that horrible dry heat. Even as the sun slowly disappeared and it turned cooler in the evenings, it was still too warm to sleep inside, so we made our beds out under the stars.

For miles around Al-Tash camp, there was nothing but dead land, but in the gardens of our mud houses, there was life. People grew grass, and planted and watered trees – badly needed splashes of green in a world that was otherwise made up of different shades of brown.

And in our garden was the one thing that, more than anything, made this place feel like home for my parents: their little vegetable patch. They were farmers, so they farmed, just like our family had always done in Zahaw.

THE TOWN

As soon as school was finished in the morning, I would find Makwan, my brother, and the two of us would sprint off together as fast as our legs would carry us. If we had been daydreaming in class – which is very possible – there was every chance that we were wishing the time away and counting down the minutes until we could run out and get some baklava, a beautiful sweet pastry made with nuts and honey, from the little shop that sold it.

The Iraqi government wanted to keep Al-Tash camp cut off and isolated from the rest of the region. The barbed-wire fences that surrounded the camp in the early years didn't last for ever, thankfully, but even after they had been broken down, we were still restricted. Strictly speaking, anybody who lived in the camp was forbidden to go more than five kilometres beyond the boundary for any reason, but as time went on, the enforcement of that rule became more and more relaxed – unofficially, at least. Still, every time we tried to leave the camp, there was a chance that we could be turned back. The local police sat in their station on the side of the road at the entrance to the camp and watched everybody as they came and went. It was always the same two policemen for as long as I can remember. They knew everybody, and everybody's business. Depending on who you were and where you were going, or what mood they were in, they might be happy to turn a blind eye and wave you through. If not, a little cash – a bribe – would encourage them to look the other way while you went about your business.

Over the years, we created a little economy of our own, with all the shops and services we needed right there in the centre of the camp. To us, this was 'the town': our market, our community centre and our meeting place all in one, a long narrow strip about a ten-minute walk from our house – less if Makwan and I ran. The huts and stalls lined both sides of the road, their owners sitting out the front under canopies propped up by pieces of timber jammed into the ground. No matter what time of the day it was, there would be hundreds of people in the town, young and old, standing and chatting and buying and selling. We'd be on the hunt for freshly made baklava, but you could get practically anything you would want or need. Boxes of vegetables sat open on the table tops, beautiful green cucumbers and

36

fresh red tomatoes laid out to grab the eye of whoever was passing by. Lambs and goats, already butchered and trimmed, hung from metal hooks at the shop front. Chickens squawked in their cages, alive for now but only until the next customer came along.

Whether it was selling fruit or vegetables or meat, or stitching clothes or mending shoes or cutting hair, these had been people's livelihoods before they became refugees, and they would still be their livelihoods when they could finally leave to start a new life somewhere else. If we were buying meat, we liked to get it from one particular butcher – and we still do, even today, because that same man is still a butcher and has his own shop in Dublin now.

Once the baklava had been demolished, Makwan and I would go to visit my brother Osman at his vegetable shop. He might give me a job, cleaning up the fruit and vegetables that he had brought back from the big market in Ramadi that morning and separating them out into different boxes for him. I'd watch as he filled his big thick notebooks with the details of what he had sold and for how much. The price of anything was never set in stone so there was always a back-and-forth, the customer looking for a discount or a little bit extra:

'I'll have one kilo of tomatoes, please.'

'Of course. That will be 200 dinar, please.'

'Oh no, come on. For one kilo, let's agree 150 dinar, and then I'll come again and buy from you the next time.'

'I can't sell one kilo for 150 dinar. They cost me more than that to buy.'

'Okay, well, if that's the price, maybe you can add in a few more tomatoes for me, and I'll still come again the next time?'

I would watch as this went on and on, Osman giving a little but also making sure that he got a little in return, until the deal was negotiated and the customer walked away happy with their bag of tomatoes. Then the next person would arrive and it would start all over again.

There were others who would come to speak to Osman quietly, trying not to draw too much attention, explaining that they didn't have any money that day, and asking if it would be possible for them to pay him back some other time. Osman would open his notebook again, writing 'I gave Mohammed a kilo of cucumbers and a kilo of tomatoes.' Everybody knew each other so they trusted each other to do the right thing, to look after each other when things were a little tight and to repay any debts when things got a bit better again. It could be months before Mohammed paid Osman, and some people would never be able to pay him. After a while, he would just draw a line through their name in the notebook and say, 'Ah, he paid me,' and that would be the end of it.

Although there were butchers in the town, most people didn't eat a lot of meat because it was very expensive. At home, I loved the smell of freshly baked naan bread as it filled the house. I would watch my mam and my aunties hard at work for hours, kneading the dough and then baking it in the tandoor oven. It was so fresh and so delicious that I didn't even want any meat or salad to go with it. I would just eat it straight, still hot from the oven. Naan bread and a cup of tea, and my stomach was happy.

My family could probably have afforded to eat meat once a week, but we didn't. If we ever asked if we could have a barbecue in the garden, my parents hesitated. They knew that there were families living near us who would only have meat once every two or three months, because that was all that they could afford, and they felt that it wasn't fair to have the smell of meat wafting up the road while we enjoyed ourselves.

A lot of other families felt the same way. Not everybody living in Al-Tash camp was broke and struggling. There were a lot of wealthy families who had managed to hang on to their money and their gold, or families who had a very busy shop and were doing well for themselves. But they all knew that at the end of the day, we were all refugees, we were all at the same level, and we were all in the same situation for now. No matter how much money the family had, or used to have, all of us children went to school together and they wanted every kid to be the same.

It was the same when it came to clothes. My parents would have had enough money to buy me a nice new tracksuit three or four times a year if they wanted to, but they didn't. Instead, in a big family like ours, the clothes would be passed down from brother to brother. If they ripped, we brought them to the shop in the town to get them stitched up again, and we'd keep passing them along until they were completely worn out and ragged.

I loved the big celebrations every year – Newroz, for the Kurdish new year, and Eid Mubarak for the end of Ramadan, the Muslim month of prayer and fasting – because they were the main times when we were allowed to have new clothes. Most others in the camp were the same. Everyone waited and saved and put their money away so that they could buy a few new things and have the whole family dressed nicely for the occasion. The men might wear the same trousers all year so that they could afford a new chokho-raanak, the traditional Kurdish outfit with the waistcoat and trousers, and the women would buy a new dress. After that, they might not buy new clothes again for another six or eight months.

If I was lucky, every couple of years I'd get a new pair of runners that I would be showing off for weeks to come. All our friends would gather around, asking 'What did you get for Eid Mubarak?', and we'd admire all the nice new shirts and jumpers and jeans and runners. Whenever I had new runners, I minded them like a baby. I'd wear them to school, but I'd make sure to take them off if we were going to play football; I'd prefer to play in my bare feet than to run the risk of scuffing them or getting them dirty. I could hear my mam's voice in my head: 'Be careful with your runners. You have to mind them, you know you don't get them every week.'

We might not have had much, but from a young age we were taught to respect the things we did have.

UP FOR THE MATCH

Sport has given me so much in life. Every job I've ever had, I found through sport. Most of the friends I've made, I've made through sport. It has given me a sense of belonging, and a sense of pride in being part of something bigger than myself. But I didn't start out playing sport for any of those reasons. I played because I loved it.

In Al-Tash camp, any space could be a pitch or a court or a track – and there was no shortage of spaces. We'd race each other from one end of the road to the other, running through neighbours' gardens, climbing over their walls, watching our step as we went to make sure that we avoided their dogs. For volleyball, all we needed were a couple of big sticks to plant into the ground, and a long piece of wire to run across the top between them to mark out the line of the net. If we couldn't find the sticks or the wire, or if we didn't want to play volleyball, we'd make a court and kick the ball over and back instead – 'Squares' as it was called when we played it in Leitrim years later, marking out the lines with chalk on the ground rather than by dragging our feet through the dirt.

But the number one sport in Al-Tash camp was soccer. The hardest part was picking the teams; at times there could be fifty kids there and nobody wanted to be left out. Somehow we always managed to figure it out without any rows, subbing in and subbing out so that everybody got a chance to play until we all went home filthy, exhausted and happy. We didn't need grass or boots – we played in our bare feet on the mucky ground most of the time. As long as there was a ball, we had a game. If the ball started to go flat or if it burst, somebody would take it home with them so that it could be stitched and restitched and brought back to life. All it needed then was a bit of air, and it was ready to go again for another game the very next day.

Soccer brought the camp together in a way that few other things could. Each clan had its own football team, and every year they would play each other in a big tournament. The final was always massive, the kind of game that people would be looking forward to for weeks in the lead-up to it, and then discussing or debating for weeks afterwards. It felt like the entire camp was there to watch those big games, with maybe three or four thousand people crowded in around the edges of the pitch, everyone trying to find the best spot to see the match. Those were incredible days.

I was far too young to play in those big games, but all my older brothers played for the Qadri team. If you wrote it out, the team sheet would have looked like a massive family tree – everybody was related somehow, all fourth and fifth cousins. We went to watch a match one day when Raoof, my eldest brother was playing. He jogged over to take a corner and just as he struck the ball, a big gust of wind came and caught it in mid-air, looping it over the keeper and straight into the goal. I had never seen anyone do that before. There was mayhem on the sidelines. Nobody could quite believe it – even Raoof must have been a bit shocked himself, even though he'd probably try to convince you that he meant it all along and knew exactly what he was doing. I was bouncing with pride: that was my big brother who had scored from the corner!

The tournament was fiercely competitive every year. In the weeks leading up to the first matches, each team would be trying to suss out the opposition to see who the strong teams were. One year, the Eliassis were good. The next year, it might be the Babajanis. Every year it was different; a team could have one or two great players that made them the favourites, but by the following year, word went around that those players' families had moved to Europe, and everybody knew that team wouldn't be quite as good any more.

That competitiveness didn't stop on the pitch either. Some clans were very close and got on well, but others weren't exactly the best of friends, and if the referee or the linesmen made any borderline decisions in one of those matches, it didn't take much to start a row between the supporters. There were plenty of times when I saw murmurs of frustration get louder and bubble over, and then words of disagreement turn to fights.

Nothing brought the camp together quite like soccer, and nothing divided us quite like it too. But no matter what had happened, by the next day it was always forgiven and forgotten.

OLD FRIENDS

Whenever my dad left to go to work, we were never too sure when he would be home again. He could be gone for days at a time. He worked as a bus driver in Ramadi before he got a job with an oil company, driving one of their tankers all across the country. I'd watch for the big tanker returning back to the camp, knowing that it was him and feeling so excited to see him again.

Before he set off on his next job, Dad would drive the tanker back into Ramadi to fill it up with water to bring back to the camp. I loved going with him, climbing up into the cabin and sitting alongside him, looking out of the window and asking all sorts of questions on the twenty-minute drive back into the city. Going to Ramadi was such a novelty – going anywhere was – but the moment that we drove out of Al-Tash camp, I could see that our lives weren't like everybody else's. It was obvious that we were the poorest of the poor.

Ramadi was like something from a different planet. As we got closer and closer, I could see the beautiful houses that people lived in. They were built from stone, not mud, like our houses, and they were five times bigger, if not more. To me, they were mansions. How many rooms must there be in a place like that, and what would you even use them all for? Anybody who lived in a house like that surely didn't have to choose between turning on a light in the evening and turning on their air cooler.

Even the cars on the road in Ramadi were different – big powerful jeeps that looked like they had only been bought yesterday. The people were not like us either. They looked like rich people, wearing their perfect cloud-white *dishdashas*. They were Arabs. They had the good jobs. They had power. I loved going to Ramadi, the adventure of the trip and spending time with my dad, but it made me sad sometimes too. These people's lives looked so nice. Why couldn't our lives be like that too?

We would drive down to the side of the Euphrates River and I would watch my dad as he worked, filling up the tanker with water first to rinse out the tank and the pipes, and then filling it again with fresh water to take back to Al-Tash camp where we would share it out among anyone who needed it.

Once every five or six months – provided we were

allowed by the police – our family would go to Ramadi together and we'd walk through the city and look around for a few hours and maybe do a bit of shopping. I'd always look forward to those days, but at the same time I could tell that we weren't welcome. When we walked down the road, it was obvious that we weren't from there; we looked different from the locals, and we dressed differently too. I had heard from people in Al-Tash camp that a lot of Arabs didn't like Kurds. It was more than just a dislike, and whenever someone told a story about Arabs and Kurds it was meant as a warning. I could tell that there was a real fear – we Kurds were terrified of these people and what they might do to us. I don't remember there ever being any actual trouble as we walked around Ramadi, but I could feel people's eyes on us, and it made me nervous. I was sure they could tell that we were the refugees from Al-Tash camp. I was certain that they knew we were Kurds.

I knew as well that, no matter what people said, it wasn't true that all Arabs hated the Kurds. My dad had Arab friends who were very good to our family. One of them, a lovely man named Sheikh Naji, would come to visit us in Al-Tash camp all the time. He'd pull up in this great big Land Cruiser or a pickup truck, his arms weighed down with food for us. His family were part of one of the big Arabic tribes. 'If any Arabs, if anyone gives you any hassle,' I heard him tell my dad one day, 'don't be afraid to come and look for me.' I knew then that he was a very powerful man.

Keeping in touch and making plans to meet wasn't easy in general. There weren't many telephones – we didn't have one in our house – and no mobile phones at all. A lot of the time, things were done by word of mouth: you bumped into somebody in town, the two of you made a plan there and then – 'Next Thursday night at eight o'clock, you come to our house for dinner' – and everybody stuck to it. If you made that sort of arrangement, you made sure that you were at the meeting place at the time you said, and if your guest couldn't make it for whatever reason, they always found a way to send word. They would find somebody who was travelling to Al-Tash camp, or somebody who knew somebody who was, and the message would get passed along the line until it arrived at the door of the house: 'Tell him I was asking for him and his family, and that I'm very sorry that I can't make it this time, and that we'll rearrange.'

My dad and my uncles travelled all around Iraq with Sheikh Naji, visiting different parts of the country that it would not have been safe for them to go to otherwise. He helped our family as well in a lot of ways that I never knew about until years later. At the time, refugees in Al-Tash camp weren't allowed to own a car, so any time my dad or one of my uncles bought one, Sheikh Naji would fill out the paperwork and register it for them in his name.

Over the years, after we left the camp and moved away, my family lost contact with Sheikh Naji. My dad and my uncles never heard from him, and they had no way of knowing where to find him. One of my uncles in particular never forgot Sheikh Naji and how kind he had been to our family when we needed his friendship. He wanted to see him again. And so, twenty-five years after they had last met, my uncle decided to try to find Sheikh Naji. My uncle had heard that he was now living in Başûr, the Kurdistan of Iraq, and went looking for him there to see if he was still alive and how he was doing. When he got there, my uncle managed to track down Sheikh Naji's son where he was living. He was an adult now, probably around forty, but he remembered my uncle and their visits to our house in Al-Tash camp when he was only a teenager. Sadly, he told my uncle, his dad had passed away in 2014, and then he told him the most incredible story.

A few months before he died, Sheikh Naji had travelled to the Kurdistan of Iraq in search of our family. That was his dream, to seek out this connection from his past and for everyone to meet again one last time. He travelled around the border between the two Kurdish regions, remembering that our families had originally lived close to there, and asked everyone he met if they knew where he could find us.

But no matter who he asked or where he tried, nobody could help him. Sheikh Naji never found us. Our families are in contact now through my uncle and Sheikh Naji's son, but Sheikh Naji returned home not even knowing if his old friends were still alive. A few months later, he sadly died, but my family have never forgotten him and the great friendship and kindness he showed to us.

SADDAM

Growing up, I wanted to be Saddam Hussein. Almost everybody did.

To the rest of the world in the 1990s, he was a dictator, a warmonger and an unapologetic danger to the peace and stability of the Middle East. To us, he was God.

We didn't know any different, and if we did, we were too afraid to even think the thought, never mind actually say the words out loud.

From men and women in their seventies and eighties and older, all the way down to children of four and five who were just beginning to understand the world, we loved him because we were taught to love him, and told that we loved him, every single day. Saddam was the fearless leader, the true Iraqi hero, the protector, the saviour. He was at the centre of everything, from the moment we woke in the morning until we went to bed at night. We became so used to seeing his face and hearing his voice that it felt unusual when we didn't.

Our school in Al-Tash camp had to make do with the basics, but even more essential than the pencils and paper was the portrait of Saddam that hung in every classroom. When we took out our schoolbooks, there was a picture of him on the front; inside, the pages were filled with stories about the many great things he had done for his people and the joy and happiness he had brought to Iraq. And while we learned about him, he looked down over us, always there.

When we turned on the tiny little TV at home, it was Saddam 24/7. Hello and welcome to the news: Saddam is our hero, Saddam is our idol, all hail the great and wonderful Saddam. The newspapers were the very same; a day wouldn't go past that he wasn't front and centre. On the radio, you had a choice: you could listen to people talking about how great Saddam was, or you could listen to people singing songs about how great Saddam was. There was no place for discussion, no time for debate. Criticism, even mild disagreement, simply didn't exist – and why would it? The media belonged to Saddam and his family.

For me, and for children of my age, he was the one true celebrity. He was the one we idolised. Saddam was the richest person in the world, and we dreamed about what it would be like to enjoy just a fraction of his wealth, a taste of that luxury, even if it was only for a day. Imagine what it would be like to live in a palace like Saddam does. Imagine what it would be like not just to own one palace but to own so many that you could sleep in a different one every night if you wanted to. Saddam drove the biggest, most expensive cars. He had gold chairs to sit on, and a bodyguard to stand behind him while he sat. There were statues of him. We admired his hat, his moustache, the white suits that only he could wear, his style that seemed to be ten or twenty years ahead of everyone else. He was just so … cool.

We didn't know what propaganda was. We didn't know what it meant to be brainwashed. We didn't know that the world we were living in was fiction, a fairy tale, a piece of pure invention by Saddam. For us, it was reality.

I was young, and what I didn't fully appreciate until I was a little bit older and we had left Iraq was that people were terrified. Saddam ruled with an iron fist and had built the entire country on fear. He famously used to say, 'If your TV is broken, just stick a picture of me in front of it.' It was a comment about how he felt people should be spending their free time but it was also a reminder: I'm there, I'm watching you, even in your own home.

My parents spoke positively about Saddam for as long as they lived in Al-Tash camp, but it was fear, not fondness, that made them do that. It was too dangerous for them to do otherwise. They hung a big framed picture of Saddam on the wall of our house where anyone who ever came to visit could see it. If you went to any other house in the camp, you would see the very same thing. It wasn't enough to support Saddam privately or silently. You had to make it obvious. You couldn't afford for there to be even the slightest doubt about how you felt or where you stood.

Saddam knew that he couldn't even trust his own family and friends, and he made sure that the rest of Iraq felt like that too. Everywhere we went and everything we did, we knew that the Mukhābarāt, Saddam's intelligence agency, were watching. The government knew what you ate for your breakfast, what you had for lunch, what time you left for school.

We wouldn't even dare to speak about Saddam when there were visitors in the house, even if they were people we knew well, people my family would have considered close friends. Even though they were Kurdish just like us, even though they were refugees too, there was always a chance that they might be Mukhābarāt. They might be a *jāsūs*, a spy. One word about Saddam, however innocuous, could be enough to land an entire family in prison, or worse.

Sometimes it was obvious that a person couldn't be trusted, that they were being paid by the Iraqi government to report back to the police. A family might suddenly have a nice new car when it was clear that they couldn't have afforded it. There would usually be a story – a relative in Europe with a new job who had sent some money back, or something similar – but from that day on, everyone knew to be on their guard. The real explanation was likely to be a lot more straightforward than that.

When you have been brainwashed for that long, it can be very hard to change. I still hear it sometimes now among some Kurdish refugees, long after Saddam fell and the full scale of his atrocities were laid bare for everyone to see: Yes, he was a monster who committed unspeakable crimes – but in some ways, he was good to us too, wasn't he?

HALABJA

We could hold a day of remembrance every single week from January to December, and still not have time to properly commemorate our dead; that's how many atrocities have been committed against Kurdish people through the years. That's how much we have suffered.

It's impossible to put an accurate number on the Kurds who were murdered by Saddam Hussein as he tried to suppress their fight for freedom and independence in Iraq. When he finally stood trial for his crimes in 2006, Saddam and his co-defendants were charged with war crimes, crimes against humanity, and the genocide of at least 50,000 Kurds and the destruction of at least 2,000 Kurdish villages. The true number of the Kurdish dead is likely to be many times higher than that, as high as 180,000 or more. Saddam's trial for his Kurdish atrocities was still ongoing when he was found guilty on separate charges of ordering mass executions in the Shia village of Dujail in 1982. He was executed by hanging on 30 December 2006. The remaining cases against him were dropped after his death; he never faced justice for his crimes against the Kurds.

I didn't know anything about Saddam's crimes until after we had left Al-Tash camp for Ireland and my family could finally speak freely, but nobody was spared this horror. Virtually every Kurdish family had a relative who was murdered by Saddam and his accomplices in the late 1980s, their bodies left lying in unmarked mass graves all across Iraq. They called this genocide the *Anfal* campaign. It was led by Saddam's cousin, Ali Hassan al-Majid, one of his right-hand men. It was al-Majid – known as 'Chemical Ali' – who directed the systematic ethnic cleansing of the Kurdish people through the use of chemical weapons. In January 2010, he was hanged for crimes against humanity.

The sixteenth of March 1988 is a date no Kurd can ever forget. The most horrific of the chemical attacks took place in Halabja, a city in the Kurdistan of Iraq, not far from the Iranian border. Five thousand Kurdish men, women and children were massacred that day when Iraqi war planes bombed the city with chemicals. Another 10,000 people are thought to have been injured. Some were blinded, others left with serious breathing difficulties from the suffocating damage the gas had caused to their lungs. Even now, more than thirty years later, so many of the survivors still carry the physical scars of Halabja with them every day.

My family lived near Halabja at the time of the genocide in 1988. In November 1986, after four years in Al-Tash, they slipped out of the camp one night with no intention of ever going back. They moved to the Kurdistan of Iraq, along with some of my dad's brothers and their families, and settled in a little town called Zarayan, not far from Halabja. They had a nice house there, and they started to do little bits of work on it when they could. They put a new door on it. They put up some blinds. They thought this might be a place where they could stay for a long time.

When Halabja was attacked, some people escaped the gas and fled to wherever they could find safety. Some made it to Zarayan, terrified, not knowing where their friends and family were or if they had survived. My family didn't know these people, but they knew what they could do to help and they opened their home to them. About thirty people took shelter with them in the aftermath of the attacks. They stayed in my family's house for two or three days, and then they moved on again.

Nobody knew where the Iraqi army would attack next, and the fear was that Zarayan could be their next target. My family, along with everybody else living in the town, went to the only place where they knew they would be protected: the mountains, our friends. Every morning in the days that followed, a few hundred people would leave Zarayan and go to the mountains to hide there for the day. When night came in, and as the temperatures started to fall, they would return to the town under the cover of darkness to sleep. The Iraqi planes could only bomb what they could see, and at night, it was virtually impossible for them to pick out a town like Zarayan from the sky. It was safe, if only for a few hours.

My family lived in Zarayan for two years. They built a good life alongside the Kurdish-Iraqi community that was already settled there, until the authorities realised that they weren't from there and that they were in fact Kurdish-Iranian refugees. It would have been easier to leave them where they were, but that was a risk the Iraqis weren't willing to take. Although the United Nations had negotiated a ceasefire in the Iran–Iraq War, and the fighting finally stopped in the summer of 1988, the threat of *jāsūs*, Kurdish spies, feeding vital security information back over the border to Iran, couldn't be ignored. The authorities weren't willing to let Kurdish refugees settle anywhere they liked. They wanted to keep them all together in one place, to know where they were, to watch them.

In November 1988, the Iraqi army trucks arrived for my family again. They were taken back to Al-Tash camp.

MISSING

I still see Al-Tash camp in my dreams. Sometimes they're good dreams, about my family and my friends, the people I've missed for a long time now, and the happy memories that we managed to make for ourselves in spite of everything. Sometimes they're bad dreams, of the memories that you'd rather forget, the crack of the teacher's stick all because you didn't know the answer to a question or because your maths didn't add up.

When I was younger, I was terrified of the police – everybody was. If we saw either of the camp's policemen coming down the road in the distance once every few months, that was too often. Thankfully, we didn't have much need for them in the camp, because there was never much crime or violence. We had three dogs at home, one who sat outside the front of the house and two who sat in the back garden. They weren't afraid of anyone and they always knew where to be. They were our security, waking us all with their barks if they heard the sound of someone nearby in the middle of the night, but it was never anything more than a car driving past on the road outside.

People had arguments and disagreements, of course, a few words or a little row at a football match – nothing out of the ordinary – but even though there were 12,000 of us, this was a small community where everybody knew everybody. No matter how desperate you were, if you robbed something, you were robbing from your own friends and family. We were all Kurds, we were all in the same situation, and we had all gone through enough already without adding more trouble and complications to our lives. If anyone did steal something, the whole camp would know about it in the blink of an eye. Everyone would know what you had done. The shame was worse than any punishment.

We were refugees in a country where Kurds were being killed. We needed to stick together and look out for each other, because we could be sure that nobody else was going to. When the police did come into the camp, they weren't there to protect us. They would walk through the town, and the people who had shops and stalls would give them free food, just to keep them moving and keep them away. The farmers who had built up a little flock of sheep or some other animals lived in permanent fear of hearing the lorry come down the road. Because the police knew everyone's business, they knew who was doing well for themselves, and these were the people they targeted. If a farmer had ten sheep at home, he was constantly waiting for the day when the lorry and the police would arrive and pile maybe nine sheep into the back, and take them away to where they could be sold. There were no questions asked and no explanations given. The police did it because they could, and because they knew that the farmer was powerless to do anything about it. *Tahrib* – smuggling – was the Arabic word that people used for this.

We were treated very poorly, but at least in the camp there was an element of safety in numbers. The horrible reality is that a lot of the people who went outside the camp, often in the hope of trying to find a little bit of work or make a bit of money, went missing. They were never seen again.

One way in which people tried to make money was what we called *jazeera*: they would fill bags and backpacks to the brim with sweets and lollipops and travel around to the different rural areas in the region, hoping that they could sell enough to make a little profit to bring home with them. They would say goodbye to their families and head off for a few days at a time, maybe even a week or more, travelling to as many different villages and nomadic Arabic settlements as possible until their legs were exhausted and their backpacks were empty.

My dad, my uncles and my cousins went on *jazeera* a few times. It wasn't easy, or even safe, work but any money they were able to make would go a long way back home in the camp. When they arrived at a settlement in the evening, they never knew if they would find somewhere to sleep; but the Arab families who lived in these places were so generous in offering them a place to rest, even though most of those areas were Saddam Hussein strongholds and places where Kurds – especially Kurdish Iranians – wouldn't always be welcomed. It was on *jazeera* that my dad and my uncles first met Sheikh Naji and became his friend. The next time they were passing through the area where he lived, he invited them to stay in his house.

For as long as these people were out on the road, their loved ones in the camp would wait, worried, for them to come back again safely. If they weren't home on the day that they had promised, if a week went by without any news of where they were, the worry quickly became a panic. A week could turn into a month, and a month could turn into a year, and there would still be no sign of them. Nobody had any idea of where they had gone or where to look for them. These poor people left behind devastated parents, a wife, children who would never truly know what had happened to them. Whether they had been kidnapped or murdered, they never came home.

HOPE

any mornings, I walked with my dad to the edge of the camp, where we'd meet his friends and we would wait for some news. My dad and his friends stood patiently, chatting, passing time while I listened to their conversations about places like Europe and Australia and New Zealand, and the lucky people they knew who lived there now. They waited, hoping that this would be the day when they got an answer to their question: who's next?

In among the mud houses, there was only one brick building in all of Al-Tash camp, and it belonged to the UNHCR – the United Nations High Commissioner for Refugees. It wasn't how you might imagine a UN building would look: a single storey of yellowish-white bare walls with a few small windows, and a couple of trees dotted in the dirt around the perimeter wall. Up on the flat roof, the

UNHCR flag, blue on white, fluttered in the wind, and the letters UNHCR were painted across the front of the building. It was nothing flash or fancy, but to us it represented the height of luxury, as big as ten of our houses or more, and the kind of place that we might dream of living in some day. I was one of the lucky ones. Not only had I been inside it; some nights, I was allowed to sleep there.

My parents had been in Al-Tash camp for a year, maybe two, when the UN arrived. Up until then, their safety and the standard of living in the camp was entirely at the mercy of the Iraqi government, whose main concern was how they could defeat Iran and win the war, not the wellbeing of the tens of thousands of people who had been caught up in the collateral havoc. When the UN arrived, the people in Al-Tash camp felt for the first time that they had a bit of protection, that somebody was looking out for them. They no longer felt as if they had just been abandoned and forgotten in the desert where anything could, and did, happen. They trusted the UN to be their direct line to the eyes and ears of the rest of the world – and, just as important, they knew that the Iraqi government would realise that too.

My mam's cousins were among the first families from Al-Tash camp to be assigned official refugee status by the UN and resettled in a new country. It was in the mid-1980s when they left to start a new life in Sweden. Over the years, we all became very familiar with the process: the constant stream of applications to the UN; the excitement of a family being called for an interview; the nervousness of waiting to find out if they had been successful; the mystery, a lot of the time, of the new country that they were going to. Where was this place? Would the people be nice? What was the weather like there?

Even for those families who had been accepted for resettlement, who had been given a destination and a departure date and told to say their goodbyes and pack their bags, there was still a fear – with good reason too. Until they stepped off the plane in their new country, there was still so much that could go wrong. They could arrive at the bus only to find that their name wasn't in fact on the list. It only took a moment for the police or the Mukhābarāt, Saddam's intelligence agency, to find a complication, the kind that would prevent them from leaving the camp and could only be resolved by getting the right amount of money into the hands of the right people. Even after the final goodbyes, buses had been stopped, turned around and sent back for no good reason at all.

For every family the UN managed to resettle, there were ten more desperate to be the next ones chosen. Waiting for any crumb of an update was the hardest part. Mokhtar, one of my older brothers, had a job working for the UN; he was the receptionist in the building, and also worked as a translator with the Kurdish families as they came in for their interviews. When he left work in the evening, people would be waiting outside the front gate to speak with him and his colleagues, hoping for any sort of news on where their case was in the queue.

Mokhtar would help in any way he could, but after a while, there were so many questions from so many people waiting outside that he started to sleep in the UN building at night. We might not see him at home for two weeks at a time, and even then it would be a very quick visit. He'd go back to work the next day and would do the same thing again, hardly leaving the building to go out into the camp if he could avoid it.

I didn't mind if Mokhtar stayed in work. In fact, I loved it because it meant that I could go and stay there too some nights, which was a real treat. He and his colleagues would invite some family and friends to visit in the evenings. A cool breeze blew through the building, which made every room feel like an escape from the desert heat outside. There was proper air conditioning, and enough electricity to run it 24/7, along with anything else that might be needed. There were couches and sofas, even though we mostly preferred to sit on the ground in the old Iranian tradition.

They were all such simple pleasures, but to us they were rare and wonderful and everything we could have wanted. I thought Mokhtar was one of the luckiest people I knew.

THE LONG GOODBYE

My parents wanted two things above all else when they were in Al-Tash camp: to get out of there as quickly as possible; and to keep all thirteen of us together until they did. Keeping us all together was the best decision my parents ever made in their lives.

Al-Tash camp was a unique place in one important respect. War doesn't discriminate in the suffering it inflicts, so even though we were united by the fact that we were all Kurds, the camp was incredibly diverse and multicultural. There were Sunni Kurds, like our family, but there were Shia Kurds as well. There were Yarsani Kurds – my grandmother on my mother's side is from a Yarsani family – and Yazidi Kurds and Zoroastrian Kurds. At home in Kurdistan, all these different tribes and ethnicities lived in their own separate communities and there would be little reason for them to ever meet; in Al-Tash camp, they shared a life.

People mixed. They got to know each other. They lived together, worked together. They were there together for so long that they became close. They fell in love. They got married.

There was a little bit of beauty in all of the hardship. A lot of people who found love and got married in the camp would not have even met in normal circumstances. The typical Kurdish tradition is for young men and women to marry someone from close to home. There are connections between neighbouring villages, and friendships between families who have known each other for many years. Marriage strengthens those ties and makes them official. In Kurdistan, we often describe someone's partner as coming from a certain family or village; in many parts of Ireland, I've noticed a very similar thing, except people are identified by the GAA club they are from.

The weddings in Al-Tash camp were special days, beautiful celebrations for the families and the community, but for the parents involved, there was often a touch of sadness too. Marriage, and the start of a new family, made it very difficult for them to keep their family together. A daughter might decide to leave Al-Tash camp – to leave Iraq entirely – and move home to her new husband's family's village in the Kurdistan of Iran. A son and his new wife might apply for resettlement in Europe. Another son could end up moving even further away with his family.

It happened to my mam as she was growing up. She went through so much of her own life without having her family around her. She has two sisters in Sweden, another in Denmark, an uncle in England and a first cousin in New Zealand. Of course they stayed in touch as they lived their lives and raised their own families, but they don't see each other anywhere near as often as they'd like. My mam speaks to her sister in Denmark every single day, but they hadn't seen each other for thirty years until her sister visited Dublin in the summer of 2022. Life and all its various complications make it hard for families to meet in person; a lot of the time it takes a death in the family, and a funeral, to bring people back together again.

After the Gulf War ended in 1991, thousands of refugees took their chance to leave Al-Tash camp and go back to the Kurdistan of Iran. For nearly ten years, as Kurdish-Iranian refugees living in Iraq, they had been viewed with suspicion and marked out as potential spies. When they returned to Iran, the authorities there were also unsure where the returning refugees' loyalties now lay. People had to sneak back to Iran through the mountains so that they could return to their villages and try to rebuild their shattered lives. My grandparents on both sides and some of my dad's brothers went back to Kermanshah province, where Zahaw is located; it was nearly twenty years before he saw them again.

My parents could have gone back to Zahaw too, but they had already made their minds up: they wanted a new life far away from the memory of the bombs and guns and suffering. They wanted to take us – me, my brothers and my sisters – to a better place, a better environment, one where we could live our lives out of the shadows, where there would be no more fear of war. Family would always be family, and Zahaw would always be home to them, but they had already decided that, as soon as they got the opportunity, they needed to get out of the Middle East.

There isn't anything that I miss about Al-Tash camp, really, apart from the people. Our family was our life. We were surrounded by our relatives and we spent every day with them. Now, we might only get the chance to talk to them over the phone or on social media, or they might visit every couple of years. That's one thing about Kurdish people: we never really say that we're going on holidays; we say that we're going on a visit.

I have family scattered all over the world. I don't remember my grandparents on my mother's side; they left Al-Tash camp to return to Kurdistan in 1991 when I was only three months old and died before I had a chance to visit them in later life. I have an uncle and cousins in Sweden who I haven't met. I have a cousin in Italy, some in the Kurdistan of Iran, others in the Kurdistan of Iraq. One of my brothers, Bakhtiar, moved to Sweden and lives there now, but the rest of my immediate family are here in Ireland.

I know that I'm lucky to have them so close. We can never take that for granted.

Before phones and the internet, videos became our only real way of keeping in touch with family while we lived at Al-Tash camp. There was great excitement at home when we found out that 'The Cameraman' was coming. He was one of the few people in Al-Tash camp who owned a video camera and he visited houses to make videos for people to send to their relatives. The day before The Cameraman came, my brother Raoof wrote a list of all of the names of the people in the village that the tape was going to – the uncles and aunts and all their children, and any other relatives or friends – to make sure we didn't miss anybody. We would sit and the camera would go to each one of us in turn so that we could introduce ourselves:

'Hi grandfather, hi grandmother, this is Zemnako. I'm nine years old now. I just want to say hello, and I hope that you are both keeping well. I miss you and I hope that we will see you soon, God knows when, we just don't know on which planet.'

The Cameraman moved around our house, recording the different rooms so that anybody watching could see what it looked like, and then he would head off for a walk around the area, the camera still rolling. Any of our relatives who had lived in Al-Tash camp themselves always wanted to see how things had changed, what our lifestyle was like now compared to their memories, how the little town looked and if they could spot any familiar faces at the stalls where they used to shop. Sometimes we would get a video in return, either from family in Kurdistan, or from another relative who had moved to Europe, telling us all about their new life and showing us their new home. Everybody who had moved away always looked so healthy, I thought. Our neighbours would get videos from their family too, and they would invite us to visit their house so that we could all watch them together. If we couldn't be together in person, at least we had some way of keeping in touch with each other's lives.

When the time came for someone to leave the camp, there were always mixed emotions: more than anything, we were happy for them, but the bonds formed over the years were incredibly close, made even stronger by persevering together and supporting each other through suffering. Whether they were family, or friends who might as well have been family, it was no exaggeration to say that nobody knew for sure when they would see these people again, if ever.

As soon as we heard the news that a family was leaving, the long goodbye began. People called to the house to spend a last little bit of time with their friends and give them their best wishes. There could be fifty people crammed into a little house, standing room only, passing in and out over the course of the day – and this went on for weeks. Every day, different people would call in for half an hour, an hour, two hours. In some cases, they might be people the family didn't even know particularly well, but knew through a friend of a friend or a passing connection; they came to say their goodbyes too, just the same as everyone else.

The family who were leaving made sure to take care of their guests. Even if there were more people in the room than you could count, everybody was looked after with tea and sweets, or offered a proper meal, or invited to stay and join the family for dinner. Families borrowed huge amounts of money in the weeks before they left, all so that they could afford to host their guests properly. The debts they racked up were massive by Iraqi standards, but they knew that once they arrived in their new country, it could all easily be covered and taken care of within a week or two of starting work. The family who were leaving knew that they were the lucky ones. They were going to live in heaven, wherever that might be. This was their way of sharing that good fortune with the people they loved.

And on the last day, we'd gather at the front of the camp, in the place where the buses parked, to say our final goodbyes. We'd wear our best Kurdish clothes, holding back the tears as we queued to shake hands and hug and offer a kiss on either cheek, the traditional Kurdish sign of friendship and respect. There was time for everyone, and never any rush. The bus would wait, the bags already safely stowed away, until finally it was time for the family to leave.

I stood beside the bus and said goodbye to a lot of my friends over the years, but as I got a little bit older, the sadness came with a new understanding and hope. Some day, we would be the ones going up the steps and leaving all of this behind. Our time was coming soon.

PRISON

When I was ten, my dad was arrested. They came and they took him away and they locked him up. To this day, I still don't fully understand what he had supposedly done wrong or what crime he had supposedly committed – and he certainly wouldn't have been the first Kurd to be put in an Iraqi prison for no good reason at all. There was a big row at the oil company that he worked for, and my dad and some of his colleagues were in the wrong place at the wrong time. They were brought to court and sentenced to prison.

The row didn't even really concern the truck drivers like my dad. I think it was actually a dispute between two of the senior engineers, most likely a disagreement over which group was making more money. It was always about money. If you had money in Iraq, you could do what you wanted and get away with it. You could pay the police not to arrest you. You could pay the senior detective to stand up in court and change his story, to swear that you were completely innocent and point the finger at someone else, the person who had really done it. If you wanted to go straight to the top, you could bypass all of them and buy the judge.

Whatever the dispute was, the side that my dad was connected with lost the argument. If he had been on the other side, he would have been fine. There was no point in explaining that he was only a driver, that this didn't involve him. Instead, he was arrested along with his colleagues and hauled up in court for a hearing that was over in the blink of an eye. It wasn't like in Ireland where there are solicitors and barristers, and everybody gets a chance to give their side of the story and ask questions of the other side. There was no presumption of innocence or entitlement to a fair trial. The judge decided that they were guilty and sentenced them. Case closed. Take them away. Next, please.

I was old enough to know what was going on – that my dad couldn't come home because he was in prison – but I didn't fully appreciate the injustice of what had happened. Saddam's dictatorship, this brutal police state, was the only world I knew. People being locked up in prison wasn't anything unusual. It was just another part of life.

I didn't spend too much time thinking about why my dad was in prison. The only thing I cared about was when he would get out again. Every day, it was the same question: 'When's Dad coming home?'

And the answer from my mam was always the same: 'Next week, I think.'

I'd ask in the morning as I was running out the door to school: 'Is it today you said Dad is coming home?'

And my mam would reassure me: 'No, not today, but tomorrow, I hope.'

Any time we got an update on his case, or the possibility of him being released, it was good news. There was never any bad news. He was coming home soon, I was told, just not today. It was always next week or the week after or the week after.

Once a week or once a fortnight, we would go to visit him in prison. If I found out that we were going, I'd look forward to it for days, buzzing with excitement that I was going to see him again. They'd sent him to a prison in a place called Tasferat first, in Baghdad. We'd organise a little eight-seater minibus and we'd pack it full of food and pillows and anything else that we wanted to bring in to him, and then squeeze ourselves into the seats around all the stuff for the two-hour drive. We'd bring more than he could possibly need for himself; some of the other prisoners were from poorer families and were very grateful for our help. The only other thing we needed was money – if we didn't have that, we were wasting our time trying to go anywhere.

It started just outside the gate of the camp. As we passed through the checkpoint just outside the police station, the minibus slowed down just enough so that the police could get a good look at who was inside while my brother dropped a bundle of notes out of the window. The police stuffed the notes into their pockets as we drove on through without any questions. When we arrived at Tasferat, the prison guards met us at the gate to ask why we were here and who we wanted to see, and to search us, which meant more money. Sometimes we would bring some sweets as well, which never hurt our case, but the money was the only thing that really mattered. It was the same with every guard we passed between the front gate and my dad's cell. Every one of them had the power to turn us away, and every one of them had their hand out. If we wanted to stay for an hour longer, that was more money again. By the time we left, we didn't have much more than our trousers. The guards would have confiscated almost everything else for themselves.

Whatever they took from us, it was worth it to see my dad again. Tasferat was an awful place, with tiny rooms and small corridors where the walls seemed to close in on top of us as we made our way through. I looked into one cell, barely bigger than the dressing room in any GAA club, and there must have been a hundred prisoners crammed in on top of one another. There were men rattling the bars of the cell, reaching out, screaming as we walked by. There were fights, beatings being dished out and nobody stepping in to stop them. It was a relief when we got to my dad's cell, and we saw that it was quieter and he had a bunkbed to sleep in at night. More than anything, I was just glad to see him again.

After three months or so in Tasferat, my dad and his colleagues were suddenly released and allowed to return home. For a moment, everything was normal again. We hoped that would be the end of the matter, but we could never be sure. And around six weeks later, my dad was arrested again. There was a new court hearing, but it was the same old story. The judge ruled against my dad and his colleagues and sent them back to prison – not to Tasferat this time, but to a different prison: Abu Ghraib.

The rest of the world learned the name Abu Ghraib later, after the American invasion in 2003, when evidence of how US troops were torturing Iraqi prisoners made headlines. It was a massive place, built on the outskirts of Baghdad, a hundred kilometres east of Ramadi, with a reputation that would strike fear into the heart of anybody living in Iraq. We were allowed to visit my dad, just as we had done in Tasferat, piling back into the minibus to make the two-hour round trip as often as we could.

I thought Tasferat was packed, but in Abu Ghraib, there weren't just thousands of people locked up – there must have been tens of thousands. It was so big and so spread out that the prisoners were held in different sections: there was one part of the prison for criminals, and another part for political prisoners. At the time, the conditions where my dad was being held didn't seem too bad to me. He was in a part of the prison with other men who were his own age, and they had a yard where they could exercise and play football. He looked healthy. But even in later years, he never spoke to me about the reality of his time in prison, and I never asked him.

I didn't mind going to the prisons, even if they were like something straight out of a nightmare. None of that really mattered as long as we were able to see my dad and spend some time with him. And when it was time to hug him and say goodbye and close the door behind us and get back on the minibus for the drive back to Al-Tash camp without him, there was only ever one thing on my mind: when will he be allowed to come home?

FALSE DAWN

Wherever there was a little television in the camp, there were people standing around it in stunned silence that day. It was the same thing on every screen, the pictures coming in live from New York City. We might have been 10,000 kilometres apart, but the shock was immediate and the fear was real. The adults of Al-Tash camp knew the horrors of war first hand. They had seen them many times in their life. When the planes crashed into the Twin Towers on 11 September 2001, they could see their future, and they knew that war would be a part of it again.

The Gulf War had ended only ten years before, and our lives had been tough enough even in the peace that followed. Nobody wanted to see Iraq involved in another war, and the hardship and suffering that it would bring with it, but after the 9/11 attacks, they knew that Iraq would be powerless to stop it. This time, the decision of whether or not to go to war wasn't going to be Baghdad's to make. It was Washington's. Whenever I was around adults who were discussing it, I kept hearing the same thing: 'Iraq is going to get caught up in this.' The only question seemed to be when, not if.

I was only ten years old, but I could see that people were frightened. Ramadi was a Saddam Hussein heartland, filled with loyal supporters, many of whom would fight any invasion until the bitter end on his behalf. If America and its allies attacked, Al-Tash camp – barely twenty minutes outside the city – would not be a safe place for anyone.

My family watched the news every day while we waited for an update from the UN regarding our resettlement. When we finally got some good news a few weeks later, it was taken away from us again just as quickly.

In late 2001 the UN informed us that, finally, it was our turn. Our family had been given refugee status and approved to move to a new country, to a place I had never heard of and knew absolutely nothing about – a place called Ireland. It was in Europe, I found out; I knew where Europe was. Near England, someone said (but not England, they probably should have added). We were even given a date for our move, only a few weeks away. We could hardly believe what they were telling us: on 12 December 2001 we would be leaving Al-Tash camp for ever. We would be moving to Ireland.

Except we wouldn't. We couldn't leave without my dad, and as November turned to December and our departure date got closer and closer, it became clear that there was no chance of his conviction being overturned so that he could be released from Abu Ghraib. If we had had enough money, he could have paid his way out of the situation like so many other people, but we didn't. So when 12 December came, we did what we had done so many times before: we joined all the other people gathered at the front of the camp, and hugged and kissed and said our goodbyes. As the families leaving for Ireland got ready to board the bus that would take them away from here, we told them that we hoped to see them again some day – only this time when we said it, we had every reason to believe that day might come very soon.

My parents had been down this road before. They were one of the first to register when the UN started accepting applications for resettlement, and they were still waiting. This wasn't even their first disappointment of this kind. Two years earlier, in 1999, we had been accepted to move to Australia. It was all systems go – we even went and got our photos taken for our official travel documents, and then all of sudden, the UN changed their mind. While we were in the middle of making plans and getting ready to leave, we were told that our application had been rejected. The move had been cancelled and there was no other alternative for us at that time. It's hard to know exactly why they changed their decision, whether it was down to politics or money or a little bit of luck – a little bit of all three, probably. The only message that my parents got was that we didn't have any relatives living in Australia, and they wanted to prioritise cases where they could help to reunite families. There wasn't any explanation that would have made us feel better. We were staying right where we were.

So when our move to Ireland fell through, it was a familiar feeling, but that disappointment was quickly forgotten in the excitement that followed just a few months later. The day my dad was released from prison was one of the best days of my life.

The time that he had spent in prison felt like an eternity to us; between Tasferat and Abu Ghraib, it was probably close to eight months in total. Then, out of nowhere, there was news of a prisoner amnesty. My dad's case was one of those chosen, and it was decided that the remainder of his sentence was being scrapped and he would be released immediately. He was given a pardon and allowed to walk free.

When he arrived back to Al-Tash, it felt like the entire camp was there waiting for him, delighted to see him again. Hundreds of people came to visit our house, queuing up to welcome him home in person and to celebrate with our family. The local police came to visit too, sitting there drinking their tea and chatting to everyone as if it was the most normal thing in the world.

Nothing could spoil those days. My dad was finally home, and now that we were all together again, we knew that we would be moving to Ireland soon. It was like winning the Lotto. Twice.

OUR TURN

Wy e had been through the interview process so many times, but no matter what had gone before, the day of an interview was always a day of hope, and having hope was better than having none.

The preparations usually started a few days before the appointment. That was the time for haircuts and for making sure our clothes were ready – the nice new ones that we had bought for Newroz or for Eid Mubarak. We checked our best pair of runners and gave them a good scrub until the white bits were white again. If they needed to be stitched, now was the time to run up to the town with them, not the morning of the interview. We always wanted to make sure we looked our best.

Over the years, we interviewed for any country we could. A certain country might commit to taking in two hundred families from the camp over a four-year period, and so every year, fifty families would be resettled there. Some families wanted to move to specific countries, places where they already had family and friends. Other families only wanted to interview for countries in Europe, but not for Australia or New Zealand. They were too far away, and too unknown. My family didn't really mind what country we moved to. We just wanted to get out.

The whole family had to be interviewed, so when everybody was ready, we went to the UN building together and waited until we were called. A lot of the people working for the UNHCR in the camp were either Iraqi nationals or Kurds, who were able to help with translating. Once the interview started, it could go on for a couple of hours as they worked their way down through their list of questions, gathering all the information they needed to fill in our forms and submit our application.

'Why did you leave Iran?'

'Why can you not go back there?'

'Why do you want to leave Al-Tash camp?'

'Why do you want to go to Ireland?'

We were forced to flee Iran because of the war, my dad would tell them, and because we were Kurds, we were in Al-Tash camp as political refugees.

'We just want to get out of here like everybody else,' he explained, and the interviewer would keep asking questions and taking notes until they were finally happy.

When the interview was over, the waiting game started. Every day we hoped for some news, watching out for Mokhtar coming down the road in case one of his colleagues had mentioned our case to him at work. It might take two or three weeks before we heard anything, plenty of time to start imagining what life would be like in this new country, how the people would look and walk and talk and dress, whether I would make new friends, whether we would like it there. When the bad news came through, those dreams vanished into nothing. After a little while, the whole process would start all over again with the haircuts and the good clothes and the clean runners and another interview.

Except this time, it wasn't bad news. We could barely believe it. This time, we really were going. At the end of June 2002, we would be leaving Al-Tash camp, leaving Iraq, and moving to our new home in Ireland.

If there was ever a reason for a celebration, this was it. We couldn't have hoped for happier news – and yet, my parents' first instinct was to say nothing and tell nobody, at least not for the moment. After nearly twenty years in Al-Tash camp, they had seen too many plans change at the last minute, too many delighted families left disappointed. They had been through it all themselves before as well. This time, they wouldn't truly be able to believe their good luck until the door of the aeroplane opened and they set foot on Irish soil.

There was another good reason too. Once we started to say goodbye, once that genie was out of the bottle, we would be saying goodbye until the day we left. They knew how difficult that time would be for everyone, the mixed emotions we would all feel, how sad it would make us all in spite of the happiness. It wasn't until two or three weeks before we left that they finally started to tell people the news. The first visitors called to our house to see us, and before long, every night was a party as our friends and family ate together and told stories, swapped memories, and talked about what our life would be like in Ireland.

None of us knew what to expect, not even my parents. All we really knew was that we were being offered a better, safer life than the one we currently had. In our new home, we knew that we would be welcome.

ONE LAST STOP

'Is fada an turas é ó Ramadi go Liatroim', to paraphrase Seán Óg Ó hAilpín, and it started with an eight-hundred-kilometre bus journey.

With our life packed up into a couple of bags, we boarded the bus that took us out of Al-Tash camp for the final time and headed west on the road to Amman, the capital city of Jordan. There was one other family with us on the bus, as well as a girl who was travelling by herself. We were all setting off for three new beginnings in three different countries: us in Ireland, the other family in New Zealand, and the girl in Australia.

If it took ten hours to get to Amman, it felt like double that. I tried to sleep, but when I woke up, we were still miles away. When we had been on the road for a few hours, the driver pulled in at the side of the road and stopped for a break. As we got out to stretch our legs for a few minutes, a little convoy of cars pulled over behind us, and fifteen or twenty people got out of them. I realised that I knew the faces. I knew them very well. It was our cousins and some family friends. They had found out where the bus driver was planning to stop and followed us all the way from Al-Tash camp to see us safely on our way and say one last goodbye. Before we got back on the bus, we made sure to get a photo of all of us together. We didn't know when we might get the chance again.

My parents did their best to hide it from us, but they were nervous, my mam especially. We were so close now, but as long as we were in Iraqi territory something could go wrong. Until we got to the border, she half-expected to see a police car pull up alongside us and force the bus to stop and turn around, to tell the driver that there had been a mistake, that he should take us back to Al-Tash camp. Even when we got to Amman, she couldn't fully relax for fear that something might still go wrong. This was what she had wanted for twenty years; she couldn't bear the thought that it could still turn out to be the most crushing disappointment of them all.

We stayed in a hotel in Amman for a night or two while we waited for our flight. It was a Sunday and the World Cup soccer final was on the television, Brazil – Ronaldo's Brazil – against Germany. In among the non-stop Saddam propaganda, the TV stations we had in Al-Tash camp found some time to show football matches; even in a dictatorship, we still knew who the most famous player in the world was. When we were out playing, Ronaldo was the one we all tried to be like. Everyone sat together in the hotel and watched as he stole the show with two goals and a terrible haircut. Brazil won 2–0; they were the champions of the world.

It's funny the things that stay with you: we were in this big city, on the most important journey of our lives, and the thing that I remember the most is the taste of the water from the taps in the hotel. I took a drink of it, and it wasn't like any water I had ever drunk before. It was so salty.

The next day, Monday 1 July 2002, we got our things together and set off for the airport in Amman. First, we would fly to Frankfurt in Germany, and from there, on to Dublin. It was my first time in an airport. It was all new to me; the departures board, the security screening, the baggage carousels – everything. When we went to check in, my parents took out the travel document with the UN stamp on it and carefully presented it to the person behind the desk. We didn't have passports, so this was all we had, and it was even more precious: a piece of paper, which must have been A3 size if not bigger, which had all our names and photographs on it and stated that we had been given permission to travel as political refugees.

I was exhausted on the flight to Frankfurt; at that stage, we all were. It had already been a long journey, and we still had a fair way to go. When we landed, the first thing we noticed was the weather. It might have been a lovely German summer's day, but it was a world away from the dry, dead heat that we were so used to in Iraq. This place was cold.

Before we knew it, we were boarding again. When I next opened my eyes, the plane was approaching Dublin Airport. I looked out the window as the coast of Ireland slowly started to come into view. I couldn't take my eyes off it. All my life, I had lived in a place that was dry and dusty and brown – but this, this place was so green. I didn't know a place like this could exist. It was like nothing I had ever seen before.

As the captain came on the intercom and said something I didn't understand, and the plane slowly got closer to the ground, everything started to take on its true shape. The houses looked nothing like the mud houses in Al-Tash camp; they were beautiful. Everything around them was so healthy, so full of life. It all looked amazing. I couldn't wait to get off the plane, to walk outside and be in this place and breathe in the air. I could tell that we were going to like it here.

LIFE BEGINS
IN LEITRIM

When we arrived in Dublin Airport, there were some familiar faces waiting there to welcome us to Ireland. My parents had stayed in touch with the Kurdish families who had moved to Ireland the previous December when my dad was still in prison. When we realised that we would soon be following them, my parents phoned them a few times to ask how they were settling in and to find out a little bit more about Ireland and what we should expect. It meant a lot to our family that they came out to the airport to meet us. Even with all the excitement, it was still a strange feeling to finally be here. We were in a strange new place, far away from the world we knew, but when we saw them waiting there, we knew straight away that at least we weren't completely on our own.

The other Kurdish families lived in Dublin but we were going to a different place. A woman named Martina Glennon from the Department of Justice introduced herself and welcomed us. Raoof and Mokhtar were the only two of us who spoke any English, so Martina explained to them that we still had one more journey to make before we were done. The bus was waiting outside to take us to Leitrim, to our new home in Carrick-on-Shannon.

As time went on, a hundred Kurds or more would call Carrick home, but in the summer of 2002 there were no Kurdish families living in Leitrim. We were the first. There were others who had come to Ireland before us, but most of them had settled in Dublin. Our house was in Oaklands, an estate of around eighty houses a five- or ten-minute walk outside Carrick town. When the bus turned into the estate for the first time, the first thing I noticed was how organised everything seemed. These were lovely brick houses, laid out in neat rows around proper roads and nice green spaces. Every part of the estate had been thought about and planned. It was the same when we pushed open the door of the house and went inside to look around. There were two floors, an upstairs and a downstairs, and we could tell straight away what each room was used for. Everything had its place, had its space. We couldn't have imagined anything more luxurious.

Martina showed us around the house. She showed us how everything worked, told us about all the different switches and dials and buttons and what they did – how to heat the water, how to turn the oven on. We'd never had running hot water in Al-Tash camp. We'd never needed it; it was so warm that we only ever wanted to have cold showers, and that was easily done with a bucket or two straight from the well in the garden. Martina made sure that we had everything that we needed, and when all of that was done, she left us to settle in. She handed my parents the keys, and the door closed behind her, and then it was just us. We were exhausted, we were a little bit lost, and none of us really knew where to go or what to do first; but more than anything, we were happy.

We had a lot to learn in those first few months – like the fact that the word 'summer', the whole concept of it, means very different things to different people. We quickly realised an Irish summer, a Leitrim summer, isn't really like summer in other places. We were cold, for one thing, cold enough that we still wanted to wear our big coats any time we went out. And it rained a lot. Where we were in Iraq, it probably only rained five or six times a year, and for anyone living in Al-Tash camp, maybe that was no bad thing; every time there was a big downpour, it turned the entire camp into a muddy swamp. In Leitrim, we soon discovered that no matter what time of year it was, you could never truly look up at a blue sky and trust what it was telling you. It only took a moment for the clouds to come in.

When we first arrived, my parents told us that they were going out. 'We'll be back soon. We're just going to walk down to the town to go to the shops.'

'Wait for us,' Makwan and I insisted. 'We want to come too.'

It was only a short walk but everything was new to us, everything was an adventure, and we weren't going to sit at home when there was an opportunity to go out and explore. We walked down the road, checking out every shop window until we got to Paddy's, a little supermarket on the corner in the centre of the town. We were so excited. I had never been inside a supermarket before, and neither had Makwan. While my parents went looking for the things they needed, the two of us wanted to see what was in every fridge and on every shelf, looking at all the different labels as we tried to figure out what was what.

'Are we allowed to get something to drink?' we asked.

'Okay, one each.'

We raced back to one of the drinks fridges to start to figure out what felt like one of the most important decisions we'd ever make. We looked at every can, using the colours and the logos as our only guide to what might taste the nicest. In the end, since we didn't really know what anything was, we did what any smart children would do. 'One each,' we were told – nobody said anything about what size it had to be. We picked the two biggest cans that we could see and ran back to the counter to hand them to my mam and dad so that they could pay for them with the rest of the shopping.

Padraic McGoldrick, Paddy's son, was behind the till. I'd get to know Padraic through the GAA when I got a bit older, but at this stage we were just some customers he had never met before. I'd love to know what he was thinking as he saw me hand my parents a can of Guinness, and Makwan hand them a can of Budweiser, practically bouncing with the excitement. He can only have assumed that the cans were for my parents, and that we had just run back to grab them from the fridge for them, because he packed them up along with the rest of the shopping without saying a word, and we headed on our way.

As soon as we were outside, the two of us cracked the cans open and took our first sips as we walked down the road. Mine didn't taste quite like I expected, and one look at Makwan's face was enough to tell me that his didn't either. Maybe the Irish drinks were just a bit funny and it was one of those things that we would just have to get used to.

We already had the cans half-finished when a passing guard spotted us and marched straight over to speak to my parents. It was a one-sided conversation, and Garda Martin Cunniffe was the one doing all the talking. Neither of my parents had a word of English but as he pointed to the cans, and then myself and Makwan, and then back to the cans, all the while shaking his head, they understood enough of the message. We weren't quite sure exactly what the problem was – we still had no idea that it was alcohol – but my parents could see that Martin wouldn't be happy until the cans were in the bin, so into the bin they went.

I don't know if Martin could ever have imagined how his path would cross again with the eleven-year-old with the can of Guinness in his hand. In later years, when I was playing for Leitrim, and Martin was the senior hurling manager, we'd have plenty of opportunities to have a laugh about that day.

APPLE

aron McPartland was my first friend in Leitrim. A couple of days after we moved in to Oaklands, he spotted us playing football outside and came over to introduce himself.

'Hi, I'm Aaron,' he said.

'Hi,' I said. That was as much English as I knew.

Aaron said something else that I didn't understand, and when I didn't answer, he pointed to himself and then to the house two doors down from us. That was where he lived. Then he pointed to me and Makwan, and pointed to our house. That was where we lived? I nodded yes. So far, so good.

I couldn't understand a word Aaron was saying, but I saw that he had a football too, so at least we had somewhere to start from. Everything else we worked out through a series of hand gestures and sign language. Did he want to play football with us? He did? Great.

The football was like a magnet. Any time there was a little match out on the green, we met more and more of our new neighbours. Aaron's sister, Shauna, joined in as well, and when the other kids from around the estate looked out of their windows and saw us out there, they all wanted to know if they could play too. Everyone was welcome. We never quite made it to Al-Tash camp levels of fifty kids and one football, but we never had a problem finding enough people to have a game.

We made a lot of friends, but Aaron and I spent the most time together. He would come over to our house, or I would go over to his and we would play his PlayStation – well, he would play his PlayStation and I would watch, because I didn't even know what a PlayStation was. The first time in my life that I went to the beach, it was with Aaron and his family. His parents invited me and Makwan to join them on a trip up to Donegal. I couldn't believe how beautiful it was with the waves crashing in on top of the golden sand.

We still had to communicate through hand signs and pointing, but whatever we were doing, Aaron tried to help me to learn a couple of words.

'Hi, how are you?' he taught me, and I'd repeat: 'Hi, how are you?'

'I am fine,' he'd say, and I'd repeat: 'I am fine.'

If we were in his house and he was getting us something to drink, he'd pass me a Coke, and I learned that it was a 'can'. If we were hungry, he'd go to the kitchen and get us a 'biscuit'.

While Aaron was busy teaching me about cans and biscuits, my parents and older brothers and sisters had plenty to organise as they tried to settle in. In those first few weeks it felt like there was always somewhere they needed to be, or something new they needed to learn. There were appointments with the Garda National Immigration Bureau so that their residency could be officially approved, and one of the local guards in Carrick very kindly drove them up and down to Dublin as they needed. There were more appointments to get their PPS numbers, so that they could start to look for work and apply for jobs. Raoof and Mokhtar started to find work as translators; when a new Kurdish family came to Ireland with no English, they would go and meet them and help them with the language barrier while they were finding their way around Ireland and the Irish systems.

We were immediately treated to an Irish welcome in all its generosity. Great people from the community were always calling over to our house, whether it was to teach my parents a little bit of English, show my brothers and sisters how to type up a CV, or help us out in some other way. They were so important, not just in helping us to get set up for the first day or two, but in laying a foundation for the rest of our lives in Leitrim and in Ireland. They became family friends and my parents were always delighted when they visited in the evenings to have dinner with us. Even after we moved away from Leitrim, these people kept in touch to see how our family was doing, which we really appreciated.

This was our new life. So many of the worries of the past were gone; they just didn't exist any more for us in Ireland. We knew that we would have a proper breakfast every morning and a proper dinner every evening. We were safe here. It was love at first sight for all those reasons and more, but it was unfamiliar and it was strange to us and every day brought a new challenge.

We all found it difficult in different ways, but as a child it was easier for me to adjust to these new surroundings, this different culture, than it was for my parents. Of course I was frustrated that I couldn't communicate with my new friends, that I couldn't understand them and they couldn't understand me. But at least I had opportunities to make friends, which immediately meant that I was more integrated into the community. It's naturally easier for a child to learn a new language too, and it didn't hurt that I was surrounded every day by other children who were speaking English.

Even though my dad could write in three languages, he had never really had the opportunity to learn English. Initially, it wasn't really a problem; Raoof and Mokhtar were there to help with translating any of the important conversations, but as they got busier with work, they weren't always at home.

The language barrier was only one part of the adjustment. We were used to living in a Kurdish community where everybody wore Kurdish clothes every day, but now we were the only Kurds in the entire county. Again, it was easier for me. All I wanted was to fit in; I already stood out enough. I was looking out to see what the other children around me were wearing – jerseys and T-shirts and tracksuits – and that was how I wanted to dress too.

It was different for my parents; how they dressed had always been an important part of their identity and how they saw themselves. Sometimes I would see my dad wear jeans because we lived in a western culture now and in a western culture men wore jeans. He was far more comfortable in his Kurdish clothes, though. That was how he dressed most of the time, although sometimes he liked to mix and match and wear a suit jacket too. My mam continued to wear her headscarf even though very few other women in Leitrim wore one. That was how they had been brought up. That was their culture. They didn't feel the need to change, to be like everybody else in order to fit in.

Some people might look at them – wearing Kurdish clothes, still speaking Kurdish as their main language – and feel that it's wrong: that they're not making an effort or trying to properly integrate and really be a part of Irish society. As I got older, I developed a much better understanding of what integration really means. It shouldn't be about the language you speak at home or how you dress. Just because you marry an Irish person, it doesn't mean that you are integrated. Integration is about making friends, learning about the people you live with, understanding their differences, if there are any, becoming part of the community, and working together to build something.

In September 2002, I started in school. On our first day, I got dressed in my uniform, the grey trousers and pale blue shirt with a wine tie, and went out into the back garden to get my photo taken with Makwan and Reebin. The three of us were going to St Mary's National School in Carrick town. I hoped that Aaron would be going to St Mary's too so that I'd have a friend on my first day, but he was in a different school in Leitrim village.

I started off in a class with other children who were around the same age as me. There wasn't much point in me filling a school bag with lots of different books that I wasn't going to use. I needed to learn English, and I needed to learn from the start. I'd open my copybook and the teacher would print the words 'How are you?' in big, clear letters at the top of the page. While the rest of the class carried on around me, I would sit there and study those three words and the unfamiliar letters. Then I would take my pencil and try to copy the movements and the shapes until I had written it myself: 'How are you?' I would copy it again and again, fifty times, as it slowly became easier and more natural, until the page was filled. When that was done the teacher would come back to me, flip over to a new page, and write 'I am fine', and I'd start all over again.

How are you? I am fine.

We had another teacher who took me and Makwan and Reebin out to a separate room for a couple of hours every day for some extra classes. She had some books with pictures of animals, or of fruit, the kind that you might use to teach a one-year-old their first words. We learned about cats and dogs, and apples and bananas, and everything in between. We'd write them all down in our copy book: c-a-t, a-p-p-l-e. Then she'd show us the picture but cover up the word: what is that? And I'd remember: that one is an apple.

It was a slow process but every day, I remembered the words that I had learned the day before and added a few new ones. By the end of our first year in Ireland, my English had improved massively. It wasn't perfect, but I could talk to my friends and they could talk to me. Once I started playing sport as well, I felt properly at home.

HURLS AND HELMETS

C lement Cunniffe took one look at me and handed me a hurl and a helmet, the same as everybody else in my class. It was a day that changed my life.

I particularly enjoyed PE class when I started in St Mary's. It was the one time when the language barrier didn't seem so challenging. You hear people say sometimes that sport is a universal language that everyone understands – and thankfully that applied to the encouragement that my classmates were shouting at me when we played soccer. I knew what it meant when someone was roaring for a 'pass', and I had known for a long time how to celebrate a 'goal', because they're the words we use in Kurdish too. The rest of the language – 'kick', 'shoot', 'tackle', 'score' – I quickly picked up as we went along.

But then there was another sport, one that everyone else in the class seemed to know and love, but which I had never seen before. We played it with a football, but it wasn't soccer and for the life of me I couldn't understand the rules. I didn't know it but I was about to learn all about Gaelic football.

Enda Stenson was one of the first people to try to teach me. Enda is Leitrim GAA through and through. He was elected as chairperson of the county board in 2019, but back in the early 2000s, one of his many jobs was to go around different schools in the county and do a bit of Gaelic football coaching. When it came to teaching me, he decided to keep it simple and start with one of the basics: the solo. Starting with the ball in his hands, Enda juggled it off the instep of his foot and caught it again. Then he handed me the ball. My turn.

I took the ball from him and started to do some keepy-uppies. I was able to do three or four in a row without catching the ball like Enda had done, so I thought he would be impressed, but instead he looked totally confused.

'No, no, no,' he said, shaking his head. 'A solo. You only need to do one.'

I didn't have a clue what he was saying to me. I wasn't sure what I had done wrong. I tried again and soloed the ball a couple of times without catching it. Was that it?

'No,' Enda said, losing patience as he showed me again. 'You solo it – just one solo – and then you catch it again in your hands.'

He'd lost me completely now. You're not allowed to touch the ball with your hands, I thought to myself. That's a foul. But I got the message eventually. Solo. Hop. Solo. Hop. Take your point. Over the bar. Do it again.

As I got to know some of my new classmates a little bit better, I could see that Gaelic football wasn't just another sport to them. They loved it with a passion. They played it when they were in school. They played it when they were at home. They played it during the week, and they played it at the weekend. If they weren't playing it, they were talking about a match they had seen. I realised pretty quickly that if I learned how to play too, if we had that in common, I wouldn't have any trouble finding friends or fitting in. There would always be a game for me somewhere.

I saw the fuss too whenever Michael McGuinness came in to the classroom or passed us in the corridor. To me, Michael was just one of the teachers in the school, but I soon found out that he was a proper footballer. He was on the Leitrim team. Like Enda, he would come into the school every so often to do some coaching with us. Whenever he was there, I could see that the rest of the lads worshipped him. They all wanted to be like Michael. That was the ambition for them: to be a Leitrim footballer themselves some day too.

Playing for Leitrim wasn't even in my wildest dreams at that stage. How could it be? I barely knew the rules of the game. But I was having fun, and I knew that I wanted to get better, so I practised whenever I could.

And then there was the other game, the one with the big wooden sticks and the tiny little ball. Trying to learn English and trying to learn how to play Gaelic football were confusing enough until I started trying to get my head around hurling too. Clement Cunniffe is a Leitrim hurling legend now, but back then, he was just a young lad going around schools trying to get kids interested in the poorer cousin of the Leitrim GAA family. The footballers had history: 24 July 1994 was still etched into the collective memory of the county as if it was yesterday, one of the GAA's all-time great underdog stories, the day when little Leitrim – population 25,000, give or take – came in from the cold and beat Mayo to win the Connacht senior football championship. The county had been back to a Connacht final as recently as the year 2000; Michael McGuinness and his team-mates had won a minor provincial title just two years before that. Yes, Leitrim's footballers had all the history. The hurlers, by comparison, had none.

I didn't know how to put on the helmet when Clement handed it to me on that first day, and I didn't know how to hold the hurl either. He showed me how. That was how it all started.

JOIN THE CLUB

'Y ou know where the shop is, before the fire station?' Paddy McGoldrick tried to explain to me in school one day. 'That's where training is. Come up later on.'

All I wanted to do was play sport, all the time. I wasn't interested in anything else. Within a few weeks of starting school, I had joined every club I could. I played soccer with Carrick Town. I was running with Carrick Athletic Club as well. When Paddy suggested to me that I come up to St Mary's GAA and join the team that he played for, I didn't need to be asked twice. I knew where the fire station was. I'd see him there.

At that stage, I had only tried Gaelic football a handful of times in PE class. Everything about the sport was still so new to me, but that wasn't going to stop me from joining a club. I wanted to learn, I wanted to practise, and I loved the thought of being on a team, of knowing that there would be training sessions that I could go to a couple of evenings every week and then a match at the weekends. At the start, it didn't really bother me if I was any good or not. I just wanted to be out running around and hanging out with other kids my own age.

I still had a lot to learn. Every time I thought my skills were getting better, or I was getting the hang of the rules, the whistle would blow or someone would pull me over to one side:

'You can't bounce the ball twice in a row like that. It has to be a solo after a bounce.'

I watched the other lads to see how they were doing it. Okay, I understand.

'You can't throw the ball to your team-mates. You either have to kick it, or pass it with your fist – like this.'

Gotcha.

I was fit and I was fast, so I was well able to keep up, and even as I was learning, I was having fun. The first time I played a match for St Mary's, I might as well have been playing soccer. I hadn't quite mastered how to pick the ball up legally so it was easier to keep it on the ground and dribble it and then pass it to someone who could pick it up. My parents loved coming down to watch my matches. When I looked over to the sidelines, my dad was standing there with the camera in his hands, recording everything that I did. He couldn't wait to tell our relatives back in

Kurdistan about the new sport that we had found in Ireland and send them the video of me playing it.

If I wasn't at training or playing a match, I was out having a kickabout or a puck around, up in the club with Darragh Singleton and James Glancy and the rest of our friends, until it got too dark to see the ball or the sliotar or until someone came out and told us that it was time to go home. Hurling didn't come quite so naturally to me at the start. I had been kicking a football for as long as I could remember, but hurling, with the lift and the strike, was a whole new skillset. I struggled, but I had a hurl in my hand nearly every day. I must have practised striking the ball tens of thousands of times – anywhere there was a wall, I was practising. It probably took me a few years before I caught up with the rest of my team-mates and I was really comfortable on the ball, but as long as I was good enough to be a part of the team, I didn't mind.

I was very fortunate that I had so many great people to coach me when I was starting out: Barry Singleton, Darragh's dad, and Anthony Conway were my first football coaches, along with Fintan Cox and Cormac Flynn; Kevin Glancy, James's dad, and Paddy Phelan taught me most of the things I know about hurling. All those people were there for me at the start, and all of them became friends for life. To this day, if I'm ever travelling back to Carrick, I know that there's a spare bed there for me in the Singletons' house and I'm always welcome to stay; they wouldn't have it any other way.

Every club, every county, has people like these, and they know how lucky they are to have them. They are the people who make the GAA great. They are the soul of the game, the people who volunteer so much of their time and energy for the sheer love of it, the ones who keep the game alive. I look at Barry, whose family are from Tyrone, or Paddy, whose family are from Kilkenny, and I see people whose heart belongs to football and to hurling. Once you have the GAA in you, it doesn't matter where you're from originally or where you end up, you'll never lose that passion. It will always be a part of you.

It was Paddy Phelan who gave me my first hurl and helmet. The hurl was nearly as tall as me but it was mine; I was a hurler now. And then he handed me a jersey, a red jersey which must have been twenty years old. It had no logos, no sponsors, nothing except the crest and the three words around it: Carrick Hurling Club.

I still have that jersey at home, safely put away, the very same one that Paddy gave me all those years ago. It still means the world to me.

NEW DIRECTIONS

I loved living in Carrick. That's where all my friends were. That's where my sports teams were. It hadn't taken long, but Carrick already felt like home. So I was heartbroken when my parents told me that we were leaving.

We lived in Carrick for our first two years in Ireland – two years to the day, to be precise, because on 1 July 2004, my family said goodbye to Leitrim and moved to Tallaght.

I was thirteen years old, just starting to get settled, and I didn't want to move. I didn't know anyone in Dublin, I protested, or anything about the place. Carrick had everything that we needed, didn't it? But this wasn't about me. It was a decision based on what was best for everyone in the family, and when my parents looked at all eleven of their children, the different stages of life that we were at, and what we each needed, they felt that it was the right time for us all to move to Dublin together.

My brother Bakhtiar had just finished school that summer, and Hoshar was about to start his final year. There would be better choices of college for them, if that's what they were going to do next. As well as that, there would be more opportunities for my older siblings to find work in a big city. For me and Makwan and Reebin, as the youngest three, moving now meant that once we started in a new secondary school, we wouldn't have to move again.

My parents had lots of good reasons for their decision, but it didn't mean that I had to like it. In time, Tallaght would become the one place where I could imagine myself spending the rest of my life, but in the summer of 2004, all that I could think about was Carrick and what I was leaving behind.

I had to start all over again. We moved in to our new house in Old Bawn, and when September came, I started in first year of secondary school in Old Bawn Community School. Despite all my worrying, I found it a lot easier to settle in to a new school the second time around. It was easier to make new friends, for two main reasons: I was able to speak English now, and I was into GAA. I met Paul Hudson and Dean Hoey on one of my first days in school. We became friends as soon as they found out that I played football and hurling. I knew there were a few GAA clubs in the area but I hadn't joined any of them yet. The two lads told me straight away that they would call in for me and we could all walk up to training together. That was the decision as good as made. I didn't know if I would find a new club that I liked as much as St Mary's, but there was no need to worry; in the end, Thomas Davis GAA found me.

Paul and Dean called in to collect me, as promised, for that first football training and showed me where to go, and afterwards, I was sure I could find my own way home. I headed back in the general direction that we had come from until I came to the road where our house was – except it wasn't our house. The road and the houses all looked very similar to where we lived, but it was the wrong road. I was lost.

I retraced my footsteps, panicking a little, looking for anything familiar that might help me to figure out where I was and help me to get home. After a couple of minutes, someone out walking noticed that I looked lost and stopped to help me.

'Where do you live?' they asked.

'Old Bawn,' I said.

'This is Old Bawn. Whereabouts?'

I didn't know our address. We had only been living in Tallaght for a couple of months, so I thought about the places that we had been to and that I was familiar with.

'Do you know where The Square shopping centre is?' I asked. The Square was about a ten-minute walk from our house but I had been there loads of times, so I knew how to get there and, more importantly in this situation, I knew how to get home from there too.

'Yeah, The Square's straight up that way, up that road there.'

I'm sure that I was only around the corner from home, no more than two or three minutes away, but all the corners looked the same and I hadn't a clue where I was going. The only option was to walk all the way back up to The Square, just so that I could walk home the way I knew. It must have taken me another twenty-five minutes but I got there in the end. I made sure not to make that same mistake again.

'I don't really know where I'm going,' I told Con Deasy, my new manager, after training the next night. 'Will you give me a lift home, please?' Con lived in Millbrook, the next estate over, so he dropped me home after football training until I started to find my own way around. It was the same after hurling training too; Corky – Denis O'Donovan – would pull up outside the house to collect me on his way up to the club, and bring me back home again afterwards.

Part of my heart was still in Carrick-on-Shannon, though, and I wasn't fully ready to say goodbye to St Mary's yet. For the first few months after we moved to Dublin, I had two clubs. I trained with Thomas Davis during the week but until my transfer was officially approved, I wasn't allowed to play matches. I didn't want to be standing around on the sidelines every weekend while I waited for the paperwork to go through. I wanted to play matches. So when Saturday came, I grabbed my gear bag, said goodbye to my mam and dad, and jumped on a bus to go into town. I was barely a teenager, had just moved up to Dublin, and I didn't really know the first thing about the city centre. It was huge – far bigger than Carrick town, anyway – but it didn't take me long to work out where I needed to go. I had to find my way to Busáras first, and from there, I needed to figure out which bus would get me back down to Leitrim in time for throw-in.

That was my routine for a few months: every weekend, I would get the bus to Leitrim by myself, meet up with the team, play our game, and then afterwards, I'd stay at the Singletons' house with Barry and Darragh. I'd make sure to find Fintan Cox too at some stage before I headed back to Dublin on the Sunday. Fintan made sure that I was never out of pocket for the cost of travelling up and down. He covered any money I spent on buses or anything else and made sure that I got it back.

When my transfer came through, I had to stop playing for St Mary's, and my weekend trips became a little less frequent. I was a Dubliner now, a Thomas Davis man; I never realised that some day my GAA career would bring me right back to where it all started.

IMPORTANT LESSONS

A hand shot up in the middle of the classroom.

'Sir, who's your man with the hurl in the poster?'

'How dare you?' Mr Horan spun around, insulted by the question and annoyed at having to teach this most important of life lessons again. How many times did he have to go over this?

'How dare you ask that question? That man,' he said, pointing to the giant picture that took up most of the back of the classroom door, 'is a god. That is Brian Whelahan, six All-Ireland titles between club and county, one of the greatest men ever to pick up a hurl.'

We knew that already, of course. Mr Horan was from Birr and loved Offaly hurling, so he had told us about

Brian Whelahan a million and one times before – but now, it seemed that there was someone in the room who hadn't been paying attention, so he had to do it all again. He launched into a detailed analysis of Brian Whelahan's greatness that wouldn't have been out of place on *The Sunday Game*. By the time he had covered everything – and there was a lot that needed to be said – it was just about time for the bell to signal the end of that class for the day. We were delighted with ourselves; that had been the whole purpose of the question in the first place.

School wasn't really for me. I liked history class, where we learned about the Famine and the 1916 Rising and the War of Independence, and I enjoyed geography too, but that was it. I was only really going because I had to, and because I knew that it would keep my parents happy. Even if I could have left early, they would never have allowed me to. Education was really important to my dad in particular – go to school, pass your exams, and that will help you to get a good job. That was what he wanted for all his children, because it was what he had wanted for himself, and then it was taken away from him by the war.

Old Bawn was a good school for someone like me. There were students of all different levels and abilities there, and the teachers were good. They knew that there was no point in trying to treat everyone the same if one child wanted to go on and go to college and study to be a physio, and another had no interest in college because their ambition was to get an apprenticeship and learn a trade as an electrician or a mechanic. Sometimes a teacher would ask me what I wanted to be. My usual answer at that age was that I wanted to be a bar manager or run my own pub, but it was easier for me to tell them what I didn't want to be: I wasn't made for sitting at a desk all day. I knew I didn't want an office job.

I wasn't a messer – a bit of a chatter, maybe, but not a messer. I did just enough work to stay out of trouble and stay on the good side of the teachers. There were a lot of teachers in Old Bawn who were big into the GAA, and their classes were the ones that I looked forward to the most. There was every chance that the first ten minutes, or the last, would be taken up talking about hurling or football; that was much more interesting than scratching my head over some maths I didn't understand. When the Cork hurlers won the All-Ireland in 2005, the slagging in Mr Guilfoyle's class was fierce.

'Well now, did you see how it's done?' he said. 'Did you see how we do it in Cork? It's all in the grip: short hurls, left, right, left, right. I don't know what ye're at up here in Dublin, ye're all only one-sided hurlers. Ye'll never win anything, ye're no good at all.' There was uproar then, even though we knew that he was only having a bit of craic and winding us up.

Then there was Mr Kinnarney. He was the man in charge of the school's juvenile hurling team. The juvenile age group is under-14s, so mainly for lads in first and second year, and I signed up to join it straight away, as did Paul and Dean. Mr Kinnarney was from Offaly. He taught us science, and he taught us a lot about hurling too – The Legend, we used to call him. He was a very funny man. It was hard not to laugh at his team talks before a match or at half time. He might pick out a player who hadn't really got involved in the play in the first half:

'What are you at? *What* are you at? What are you looking for? Daisies don't grow this time of the year. Are you looking for mushrooms? I'll get you a mushroom. I'll buy you a bag of mushrooms.'

The rest of us would be staring at the ground, pretending to check our laces, anything to avoid catching each other's eye for fear that we'd burst out laughing. Mr Kinnarney would move on to someone else who he wanted to see a bit more involvement from in the second half:

'What are *you* looking to do? You look like you were picking grapes. Will you hold the hurl with two hands, and shove it up in the air and catch it and push fellas out? You're a big lad. If I had your size, I'd be killing everyone on the field.'

He was a good manager and that first year, our team got to the championship final. It was the Dublin Juvenile D Hurling championship but, for us, getting on the bus to go out to O'Toole Park in Crumlin that day, it was the biggest game of the year. We were up against Oatlands College from Stillorgan, who were a very strong side too. We were six points down at half time but we turned it around to win by two points.

There was a reporter and a photographer there from the *Evening Herald* to cover the game, and when we opened the newspaper the next week, there we were. There was a picture of us celebrating afterwards with the shield, so big that it nearly filled the entire page, and the headline 'Old Bawn Are Best'. We were delighted with ourselves, but I learned the most important lesson from Mr Kinnarney when we were back in school a few days later.

'Sure that was only a D Championship you won,' someone said to him dismissively, not realising that there was no 'only' about it in Mr Kinnarney's eyes. To us, and to him, a D Championship was as big a deal as any other.

'What have you won?' he asked straight away, already knowing the answer, and the conversation was over as quickly as it started. The other fella had no comeback at all.

'It doesn't matter what level it is,' I remember him telling us. 'Championship is championship. We all had to start from somewhere. Don't ever let anyone begrudge you and try to bring you down.'

I saw that very same pride from Mr Kinnarney in 2007 when the school won the Dublin Senior B Football Championship. It was huge for Old Bawn to win a Dublin championship at that level, and it was nearly the talk of the school for about two weeks afterwards. I'll never forget how much it meant to Mr Kinnarney in particular to see the school climb that mountain.

'Jesus, I'm here thirty years,' he said, nearly bursting with happiness. 'This is the best day of my life.'

We didn't know how lucky we were to have teachers who cared so much.

WE'LL CALL YOU ZAK

My name is Zemnako – at least, that's the name my parents chose for me when I was born. They always loved nature and so when I was born in Al-Tash camp, far away from anything even remotely beautiful, they named me after a mountain that lies along the border between the Kurdistan of Iran and Iraq.

It was in Ireland, in Tallaght, that I first became Zak. On one of the first evenings I went training with Thomas Davis, Con Deasy was having fierce trouble with my name.

'Tell me your name again there,' he asked.

'Zemnako.'

'How do you spell that?'

'Z-E-M-N-A-K-O.'

'I'll never manage that,' he admitted. 'How about we take the Z and the A and the K out of it, and we'll call you Zak?'

That worked for me. Zemnako isn't a common name in the Middle East – there are other Zemnakos, but nobody I actually know myself – and it's even less common in Ireland. People would ask me my name, and listen to me spell it, and do their very best to get it right, but they still got it wrong more often than not. I saw my name written so many different ways in match reports in newspapers: I was Zemnakoo and Zimnacho and for a long time in Leitrim, I was Zemaku and then Semaco.

I had already given up trying to correct people when they got it wrong – I'd had enough after the first hundred times – so I didn't mind if Con and everyone else wanted to call me Zak, if that was going to be easier for everybody to remember and pronounce and get right. Besides, it wasn't like they had dreamed up an entirely new name for me. Zak comes from Zemnako; the two are linked.

It stuck. Now the only people who really call me Zemnako are my family and some of my Kurdish friends. To everyone else, I'm Zak.

My skills kept on improving in my first few seasons playing football with Thomas Davis. I was studying the best players on my team and learning from them. I tried to figure out the best parts of their game, and then work on that, and I surprised myself by how quickly I learned. By the time I was fifteen or sixteen, I had been invited to join the Dublin development squad.

The Dublin development squad is exactly what it says on the tin: it brings together the best young players from all of the clubs around the county and gives them specialised coaching and training in the hope that they will continue to thrive and improve and go on to play at minor, under-21 and, ultimately, represent their county at senior level. No more than four or five years since I had first picked up a Gaelic football, I was already considered to be at that level: one of the best players of my age in all of Dublin.

It was a huge opportunity for me but within a couple of years, by the time I got to minor level, I just wasn't good enough. I didn't make the panel and my shot at being a Dublin footballer was all but over. If I have any regrets, it's that I didn't see the opportunity that was in front of me, and so I didn't give it the commitment it deserved. I wasn't like the other lads on the development squad. I hadn't grown up where the only dream was to wear the blue jersey; my childhood dreams were very different. So when the chance arrived, it sneaked up on me a little and caught me by surprise. I wasn't fully focused on football. I was too easily distracted. In hindsight, I was never going to be good enough.

It wasn't like I was out running around Tallaght at all hours of the night. I was too busy working. Even as a teenager, I was happier when I was out working than I was in school. I got a part-time job as a lounge boy up in Thomas Davis, but that meant that I could be there clearing tables, filling the glass washer, emptying the glass washer, stacking chairs and mopping floors until three o'clock in the morning, which wasn't doing my football career any good. I was picked in the Dublin squad for the Gerry Reilly Cup, the big under-16 football tournament that's held in Meath every year. There was one morning when we all met up at eight o'clock to travel to a match together, and I couldn't have had more than five hours' sleep. I was absolutely shattered, practically sleepwalking my way around the pitch. Even if I never put a foot wrong and nobody ever noticed, I wasn't giving myself a chance to perform at my best, nowhere near it.

That wasn't a one-off either. That was the norm, working late nights at the weekend and then showing up tired for training or a match the next day because of it. I was young. I wanted to make some money. I was afraid to ask the bar manager if I could finish up an hour or two early so that I could go home and get a little more rest.

I was only a kid. I didn't know any better, and my parents didn't either. They didn't really know anything about the GAA. How could they know how competitive that environment was, and that I needed to start looking after myself if I wanted to be serious about my football? Derek Hudson, Paul's dad, was the only person who really copped what was going on and tried to steer me in the right direction. The Hudsons are a GAA family. Derek knew what it would take to make it, and that it was a fine line between good and good enough, even at that young age. He could see that I wasn't doing myself any favours.

'You're not working tonight when you've a big match tomorrow, are you?' Derek would ask. 'Make sure you get home early and get a proper rest.'

I didn't appreciate the good advice that he was giving me. 'Ah yeah, no problem,' I'd tell him, and then I'd head off to work until all hours anyway.

Paul has always been one of the most naturally talented footballers I know. When we turned seventeen and moved on from the development squad, he made the minor panel while I missed out. Paul went on to win an under-21 All-Ireland with Dublin under one of the greatest managers the GAA has ever seen, Jim Gavin, and later to play senior football for the county too. I'd make it to Croke Park as well eventually; it just wouldn't be with the Dubs.

MY KURDISH HEROES

My Irish friends all had PlayStations but I never had much interest. I felt I was too grown up to be playing computer games. Even at the age of twelve or thirteen, I'd much rather be talking about the news, about what was going on in the world.

It was hard sometimes for me to just be a kid again and do the things that children normally do. I was used to being treated as an adult from a very young age. When we were younger and living in Al-Tash camp, whenever guests came over to visit, we were always invited to sit and join the adult conversation. It was disrespectful and rude if we didn't. We would be introduced to everyone, and then we would sit there and chat away for the evening. There might be fifty years between me and whoever I was talking to – a ten-year-old boy and sixty-year-old man – but we always had something to discuss.

I learned about the world, politics, wars and Kurdistan in those conversations. When I tried to talk to my Irish friends about Saddam Hussein, or about Kurdish culture, it was one-way traffic. They might pretend to be listening to me out of politeness but they didn't have a clue what I was waffling on about, or why I seemed to care so much about these boring adult things when we could be kicking a football or playing computer games instead.

Those evening conversations with the adults, first in Al-Tash camp and then later when we moved to Ireland, were where I first started to really learn about some of the great men and women who had fought for Kurdistan. The first is Qazi Muhammad. He was one of the most powerful Kurdish leaders in Iran in the 1940s, around the time of the Second World War, and the man who led the independent Kurdish Republic of Mahabad when it was declared in 1946. The Republic lasted for less than a year before Iran took control of the region again. Qazi Muhammad was sentenced to be executed and was hanged in public. Some of his descendants are my friends, and live in Ireland today.

I learned about the two main political parties in the Kurdistan of Iraq, and the two great tribes who had created them to lead our fight for freedom. The Kurdistan Democratic Party, or PDK, was founded by the Kurdish leader Mustafa Barzani in the 1940s. The Kurdistan region in Iraq gained autonomy after the end of the Gulf War, and the PDK won a majority when the first elections took place in 1992. When the Kurdistan Regional Government was officially recognised by the new Iraqi constitution in 2005 after the fall of Saddam, Mustafa Barzani's son, Masoud, was elected as its first president. Then there are the Talabanis. Their leader, Jalal Talabani, was one of the founders of the Patriotic Union of Kurdistan party, the PUK, in the 1970s. He was the first Kurdish man to be elected as president of Iraq as part of the country's power-sharing agreement, and held that office from 2005 to 2014.

The Kurdistan Workers' Party, the PKK, has been designated a terrorist organisation by the European Union and other countries, but Abdullah Öcalan, its leader, is loved by tens of millions of Kurdish people all over the world. He was born and grew up in Turkey, and helped to set up the PKK in the 1970s to enable Kurdish people to fight for the basic rights that they were being denied. He was captured in 1999 and put on trial in Turkey, where he was sentenced to death. While he was awaiting his execution, Turkey abolished the death penalty, and Abdullah Öcalan's sentence was changed to life in prison. He is still in prison today.

Qazi Muhammad, Mustafa Barzani, Masoud Barzani, Jalal Talabani, and Abdullah Öcalan: they are my Kurdish heroes. More than any others, they are the people who have kept the Kurdish cause, and Kurdishness, alive. They are the people who dedicated their lives, and suffered, for Kurdistan. To me, they are no different from any of the great leaders who fought for Irish independence, the men and women who have streets and buildings and GAA clubs and sports grounds named in their honour. Their names will always be remembered.

ANOTHER BIRTHDAY PARTY

We shouldn't have been drinking. That's why we had gone to the park, hoping that we'd be left alone, that nobody would spot us and that anybody who did wouldn't care enough to get involved. Giving out to a bunch of young lads you don't know for sneaking cans in a field is hard work when all you want to do is bring your dog out for a walk before bed.

I was seventeen. This wasn't a nightly, or even weekly, occurrence, but it wasn't the first time either. We weren't running amok; we were having a few cans of beer, that was all. I knew it was illegal, that we shouldn't have been drinking at all until we were over eighteen, but I had also started to absorb Ireland's particular relationship with alcohol. Some of my friends' parents didn't mind if the kids had a small glass of wine with dinner on a special occasion or half a lager shandy at Christmas. Their parents knew what kids are like, knew what curiosity and temptation is like, and how it multiplies when something is forbidden. They clearly felt that the best way to create a responsible attitude towards alcohol began at home, not out in a field on a Friday night.

But kids are kids, and I could see that some of those same friends had no problem taking the full mile rather than the inch they had been given: 'My parents will sometimes let me have a small glass of beer at home' became 'My parents don't mind if I'm out drinking, it's grand.'

My parents did mind – my dad especially – but I put that to the back of my mind as I took another sip.

'Lads, what are you at?' an angry voice boomed through the night and ended the party. It was too late to try to hide the cans. We were caught. I recognised the voice, and when I looked up, I knew the face too: it was one of my club-mates from Thomas Davis. And then I saw the uniform and realised that we were all in a lot of trouble. He was a garda, and this was a work call, not a social one.

There was panic. Was he going to take our names? Was he going to arrest us? Or – arguably the worst possible option for me – was he going to put us into the back of the garda car and drive us home to our parents to tell them what we had been up to?

Thankfully he did none of those things. 'Clean it all up now, lads,' he said, and it was clear that it was an instruction and not a request. 'And don't ever let me catch you out here drinking like this again.'

The next night up at training, I got it again from him. He was still annoyed with us. 'What are you playing at?' I was embarrassed, and I knew enough to be grateful that it was him who had caught us. Another garda could have decided to handle things differently and then we really would have been in trouble. When you're involved in a GAA club, there's always someone who is looking out for you and who has your back. You can act the maggot a bit, but only to a certain point, because there'll be someone there to save you from yourself before you say or do anything really stupid. If you're struggling and you need someone to talk to, there's someone there to help. That's the community, the bond of friendship, that exists within a club.

Sport is a saviour in Tallaght where there is a massive number of young people and it unfortunately doesn't take much for some of them to end up on the wrong path in life. My parents weren't blind to problems like drug use and abuse in the area. They were very conscious of the need to keep us safe from those particular harms. I know how much they worried about that, and how much the thought of it upset them. I understand completely because I saw it for myself. I made most of my friends through GAA, and the vast majority of us stuck with GAA and sports, but we had other friends who made mistakes, who got caught up in trouble, and whose lives are very different because of it. It's very easy to fall into that trap.

I enjoy a pint now as much as the next person, but I regret drinking before I turned eighteen. I don't torment myself over it – I was a kid. It was a mistake, and everyone makes mistakes – but I wish I hadn't done it. It was the wrong thing to do. I was breaking the law, and I felt guilty about that. More than anything, I felt I was letting my parents down.

I'm a Muslim, so people are surprised sometimes to hear that I drink; alcohol is *haram*, forbidden, according to the Quran. There are still certain perceptions in Western culture about the Middle East or about Muslims: nobody drinks, nobody eats pork, all women have to wear headscarves. That is certainly true in a lot of cases but it's also too simple a stereotype to reflect the far more complex reality. How can you paint billions of people with the same brush? It's just not possible.

Kurdish families are even more diverse again. Islam is the majority religion among the Kurds, but historically that wasn't the case. The Kurds were predominantly Yarsani and Yazidi before they were converted hundreds of years ago. Now, Kurdish families generally reflect the place they come from. Every area has its own traditions. A family might be Sunni Kurds or Shia Kurds – or they might be Yarsani or Yazidi or Christian, and not follow the teachings of the Quran at all – but for the most part, they're defined more by their Kurdish identity and heritage than they are by their religion.

To me, a lot of Kurdish people have more in common with Western people, in terms of their culture and how they see the world, than they do with people in fundamentalist Islamic states like Saudi Arabia. Every Kurdish household is its own democracy. I always think of it as quite like Catholic families in Ireland; some families are very strict in their faith and how they practise it; others are far less so. It's no different with Kurds. We have Kurdish family friends here in Ireland who are very devout. Every day, all day, they live their lives by the teachings of the Quran. But my family is not like that at all. It's not unusual for Kurdish people to drink alcohol, particularly among the younger generations, and even within individual families, you see differences. I see it with my Kurdish friends here in Ireland too. Some of them are the last man standing if we go to a bar or a nightclub at the weekend, never ready to leave, but then their brothers are very devout Muslims who go to the mosque nearly every day to pray and would never touch a drop of alcohol.

My dad didn't drink alcohol, as far as I know. Did he ever try it, even once? I don't know because I didn't ask him, but I would never say never. I suspect that nearly every Kurdish man has tried alcohol at some point but most of them will never admit to it because it is *haram*. If he ever did have a drink, Dad would never have let me see it because he would feel it was setting a bad example. Even as I got older, and I was legally allowed to have a pint, I could tell that he was still very disappointed if he knew that I had been down in the pub or out in town. He was strict in that way and he never softened. He never gave out to me, he never even said it to me, but he never needed to. It was written all over his face. My mam was far more relaxed and easy-going by comparison. Her attitude was very much 'I don't mind if you have a drink, but don't you dare ever bring trouble to this door because of it.'

Once I turned eighteen, I started going out at the weekends, usually on a Sunday night after work. I graduated from secondary school with a Leaving Cert Applied, but I never had any intention of going on to college. I was happy to keep working in the bar in Thomas Davis, as well as any other jobs that I could find. I'd finish work on a Sunday, get home, get changed into my shoes and a nice shirt to make sure that there'd be no problems with the bouncers, and I'd meet my friends somewhere local, or if we were going into town, I'd head for Copper Face Jacks on Harcourt Street. I'd hear my mam on the phone to one of her sisters in Sweden who had seen it all before with her own children.

'Where are you going tonight?' my mam would ask me when she saw me putting on a shirt or fixing my hair to get ready to go out.

'Just out. I'm going to a friend's birthday party.'

And I could hear her and her sister having a good laugh on the phone.

'Oh, I know it's a birthday party,' she'd say, rolling her eyes. 'It's always a birthday party. You must have fifty-two different friends, do you? Every week, you're going to a different birthday party.'

I tried to ignore the fact that it was upsetting my dad. I overheard my mam discussing it with him once. 'If you were the same age as Zemnako, if you were eighteen, you would be the very same,' she told him. 'You would never be home.'

My mam was right. My dad was brought up in a different culture in a different era. If he had come to Ireland as a teenager or in his twenties, he would have seen life differently. My eldest brothers were a lot older than me when we first came to Leitrim. They were already adults. Their attitude to alcohol is very much that they can take it or leave it: they will have a drink if they want to but most of the time they don't bother for the simple reason that they don't really like it.

Their children – my nieces and nephews – are different again. They were born here. They are Irish kids who are growing up in Irish society and, for better or for worse, alcohol has its place in Irish culture, whether that's the pints of stout on the counter in the pub or the bottles of wine sitting in a rack in kitchens around the country.

I'd still be annoyed if I thought they were drinking before they turned eighteen. They can come back to me when they're twenty-one; if they're still curious, we'll sit down and discuss it over a pint then.

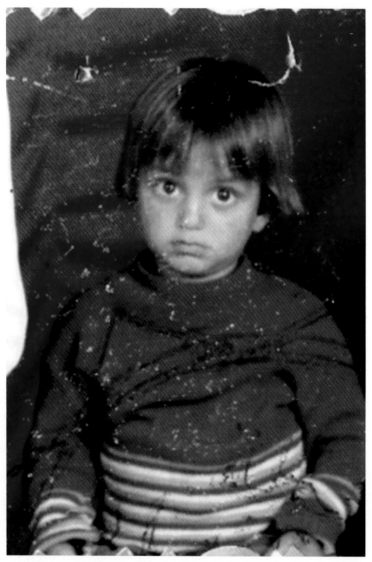

Me in 1993, aged two. When I was young, my family nicknamed me 'Kofi Annan' because I hated fighting. I still do.

The only thing I miss about Al-Tash camp is the time we spent with our friends and extended family. In this photo, my dad, Safar, is on his motorbike beside his brothers, Jawhar and Dara, and his cousins, Khassaraw and Hamid.

The family in our front garden in Al-Tash camp in 1993, not long after Makwan (far left) was born. I'm in the middle, in my brother Mokhtar's arms. The only two family members missing from this photo are Reebin, who hadn't been born, and my dad, who probably took the photo.

Newroz, 1998. The new year was a time of great celebration in the camp. My dad would wear his traditional Kurdish chokho-raanak and the rest of us would wear our best clothes.

From left to right: Makwan, Jamal, me and Reebin dressed up for Eid Mubarak in 2000.

The Qadri team ahead of the Al-Tash camp soccer final in 2001. My brother Bakhtiar is front and centre, wearing the number 15 jersey. The rest of the team was made up of our cousins and our extended family.

We were allowed to visit my dad while he was in prison in Tasferat and in Abu Ghraib. He (in the centre, in the white shirt) is having tea outside with the other prisoners. The man to my dad's left, also drinking tea with the prisoners, is a guard.

The beginning of the long road to Ireland in the summer of 2002. Some family and friends from Al-Tash camp followed us so that they could say one last goodbye when our bus stopped on the way to Jordan.

Getting settled in during our first days in Carrick-on-Shannon in July 2002. I'm in red at the top of the slide, waiting my turn.

From left to right: Reebin, me and Makwan in our uniforms ahead of our first day in St Mary's National School in Carrick. I didn't speak any English when we first arrived in Ireland, but I learned it quickly through school and sport.

Wearing my St Mary's GAA jersey as I practised in our back garden in Carrick. It took a while for me to understand the difference between a soccer solo and a Gaelic football solo.

I loved all kinds of sports from a very young age. As well as learning how to play Gaelic football and hurling, I joined Carrick Athletic Club and played soccer with Carrick Town.

Kayaking with our youth club after moving to Dublin in the summer of 2004. I look like I'm enjoying myself but I'm sure I was a bit scared too – I can't really swim that well.

LONG ROAD FROM IRAN TO CROKE PARK

Zemnakoo vows to play for Leitrim

By FIONNUALA CAROLAN

CROKE Park may soon witness an Iranian national playing Gaelic football on its hallowed turf — proving that his county can overcome its minnow status.

Zemnakoo Moradi from Carrick-on-Shannon in Leitrim has made the centre-forward position on the local under-13 side his own. And the 13-year-old hopes that his stint in St Mary's club will be the first step towards playing Gaelic football for his county.

"One of my dreams is to wear the county colours in Croke Park," he told The Star.

Last weekend Zemnakoo was part of the successful St Mary's team that won the All Ireland juvenile U-13 Competition. The win puts them through to next year's Feile na n'Og contest.

His brother Mukhtar (22) said that the whole family support him at every match.

Supportive

Zemnakoo is the only non-national on the team and started playing Gaelic football just a year ago — but Mukhtar revealed that the local community are very supportive of his younger brother.

"In Iraq he liked to play soccer but now Gaelic is his favourite sport," said Mukhtar.

Zemnakoo has eight brothers and two sisters and his parents are currently learning to speak English while Mukhtar is completing a computer course in Mohill, Co Leitrim.

When the Moradi family arrived in Dublin in July 2002 the Department of Justice sent the family to live in Carrick-on-Shannon, and Mukhtar said the family loves life in Leitrim.

"We love living in Carrick because the local people are friendly and all the children are getting a good education and learning to speak English," he said.

Zemnakoo even speaks with a Leitrim accent. Zemnakoo's younger brother Makawin, who is ten, is also learning to play Gaelic football.

The family — of Kurdish descent — have lived in Iraq but are originally from Iran.

They moved to Ireland just over a year ago after being forced to leave Iraq because of political unrest.

PLAYING BALL: Zemnakoo Moradi (13) and his brother Makawan (10) in Carrick-on-Shannon, Co Leitrim

A newspaper clipping of an interview with the *Irish Daily Star* around 2004. I was playing at Under-13 level, but even at that young age I told the reporter that one of my dreams was to wear the Leitrim colours in Croke Park one day.

Winning the Dublin Juvenile D Hurling championship with Old Bawn
Community School in May 2005. It was a huge deal for us to win any
championship, and our teacher, Mr Kinnarney, never let anyone belittle the
level that we were playing at. (© *Damien Eagers/Sportsfile*)

The best decision my parents ever made was making sure that our family stayed
together. Here, my mam meets her mam and her sisters during a visit to
Sweden in 2009 — their first time seeing each other in person in twenty years.

My mam and dad meeting President Mary McAleese at a reception in Áras
an Uachtaráin in 2009. When our family had no place to call home, Ireland
and the Irish people gave us the greatest gift of all.

Martin Cunniffe asked me to play for one season when I first joined the Leitrim hurlers in 2012. I could never have dreamed of the incredible journey that would follow over the next nine years. (© *Laszlo Geczo/INPHO*)

Thomas Davis GAA means everything to me. The club is a part of who I am. (*Courtesy of Jimmy Clarke*)

Our greatest day: winning the 2019 Lory Meagher Championship in Croke Park with Leitrim. (© *Matt Browne/Sportsfile*)

At the launch of the GAA's National Inclusive Fitness Day in August 2020. The GAA has given me so much in my life; I love that I'm able to give a little back through coaching and supporting their work. (© *Brendan Moran/ Sportsfile*)

Lining out for Thomas Davis against Cuala in the Dublin championship in 2020. Getting promoted to Senior A hurling for the first time in our history was a massive achievement for a 'football club'. (© *Ramsey Cardy/ Getty Images*)

At a campaign for Sport Against Racism Ireland (SARI) in 2022. Ireland is a place where diversity is embraced and celebrated, but there is still work to be done. (© Piaras Ó Mídheach/Sportsfile)

Celebrating with my good friend and clubmate Eoin Kirby on his wedding day in December 2018.

A very proud day receiving my Irish citizenship on 27 July 2021. To me, my identity is simple: I have Kurdish blood and an Irish heart. (*Courtesy of Department of Justice*)

Croke Park: the Promised Land. *(© Bluehueproductions)*

NO 'OTHER', JUST US

I magine this for a moment.

Imagine what it's like to be going about your day and minding your own business.

Imagine what it's like when a total stranger – somebody you don't know, somebody you've never met and probably never had the slightest interaction with – starts verbally abusing you.

Imagine what it's like for that abuse to cut right to the core of who you are, not just to try to make you feel that you are different, but that you can't and don't belong here because of that difference; that this can't be your home, that you can't *really* be from here; that you're somehow lesser.

That's the reality of life for a lot of Irish people.

Is racism a major problem in this country? No, not in my personal experience, but one racist attack is still one too many, and there are many people who have suffered a lot more than I have. Does it exist? Of course it does and, as individuals and together as a country, there is a lot more work that we need to do to tackle it and stamp it out. Have I been racially abused myself? Yes, I have. But I firmly believe that it's a very small minority who are letting the rest of the country down. They're the people who we need to teach.

There were times when I'd be going to the shops over in The Square, or walking through the park, and I'd pass a group of young lads. Sometimes they'd be drinking, sometimes they wouldn't, but there was always a group of them. None of them was ever brave enough to say what they said when they were on their own, to say it to my face when it was just me and them. They took the coward's way and waited until they were surrounded by their friends and had safety in numbers. I don't know if they remembered my face, if they even looked at it before they started mouthing off, but I remembered theirs.

Twelve years later, on a night out, I saw a face I had seen before. I went over to him and reminded him of what had happened and what he had said to me.

'What were you at?' I asked him.

'I'm very sorry, I didn't mean it,' he explained. 'I don't know what I was thinking. I was only a stupid young fella, I must have been out of my head. I'm sorry. Come here, we'll have a drink and we'll forget about it?'

I accepted his apology. I'm always happy to accept an apology, particularly if it's for something that happened when we were a lot younger. If a person recognises that they made a mistake, is willing to admit to it, and wants to apologise for it, I can understand that, because in every walk of life we all make mistakes. Nobody's perfect.

Kurdish people have gone through worse things in life than someone calling them names. My parents have seen their relatives killed and their cousins executed. That's not unique to our family; that's the experience of every Kurdish family. We have suffered genocide. It would be wonderful if the small-minded eejits could cop on to themselves, switch on their brains for a second, and stop spouting nonsense, but in the grand scheme of things, we've been forced to endure a lot worse. I would be much more worried about being on the other end of a physical attack. It's the link between these thoughts and words, and the actions that start to take root in them, that really frightens me.

A lot of the time, it seems to me that there's drink or drugs, or both, involved. When someone makes a racist comment to me on a night out, I don't even want to give them the satisfaction of letting them know that I heard them. I don't react. I just ignore it. That's the way I like to deal with it. But if they tried the same nonsense with some of my friends, they'd regret it before the words were even out of their mouth. There's no right way and wrong way to respond in a situation like that, just as there are no two situations that are the same. When I was younger it was upsetting, but now I try not to let it bother me. That person isn't going to spend hours replaying what they said over and over again, so why should I let them live in my head? That's going to annoy only one person: me. It's easier to move on.

No matter where you travel in the world, you'll meet people with Irish heritage and ancestry, whether that's first-generation, second-generation or even further back. Irish people were the immigrants once. Irish people know the pain of not having any choice except to leave a country in search of survival first, and the hope of a better life afterwards. Irish people know what it's like to be told they're different, that they don't belong, and to be abused and discriminated against because of their name, their accent, their birth cert. For some people, it seems far too easy to forget the past.

Ireland is changing every day. In the twenty years since I first moved here, the country has become a much more multicultural, much more diverse place. We might be an island but we're a part of a global economy with billion-dollar corporations and multinational workforces. We're part of a European Union that cherishes our shared freedom to move from one country to another, whether that's for work or for pleasure. In times of trouble, we open our doors to people in need.

When I started school, there was one other child in my class who wasn't white, but children now are growing up in a country where multiculturalism is the norm and diversity is celebrated. We might not be fully there yet but the Ireland I love is becoming a place where there is no 'other'; there's just us.

FAMILY AFFAIR

'Why didn't you …?'

They were the three words I dreaded the most. From the moment we got into the car, I'd be expecting them. We wouldn't even be out of the car park yet before my dad started the post-match analysis. It wasn't too bad if we'd won the game. The mistakes never mattered as much then. But if we had lost, I would be raging before he even started the engine, and then I'd have to relive every bad pass or mistimed run or snatched shot so that he could tell me what I had done wrong. I'd nearly prefer to walk home.

'Why didn't you …?'

Deep down, there was a part of me that loved those chats, even if they drove me mad. I loved them because it meant that he was there at the match, he was enjoying himself, and he cared.

My dad never really found work when we moved to Ireland. He was able to pick up some small jobs here and there, posting leaflets, but it was difficult for him because he didn't have the language. Being fluent in Kurdish, Farsi and Arabic was no real help to him here if he didn't speak English. I've always felt that if we had arrived in Ireland ten or fifteen years later than we did, his life here would have been very different. The Kurdish-Irish community is growing all the time. There are Kurdish businesses all over the country. Now when a Kurdish person arrives here with little or no English, there are a lot more opportunities for them. Language isn't as much of a barrier any more.

My parents' priority for so long had been to get us all out of Al-Tash camp quickly, safely and together. Getting out of there was the beginning, not the end. My dad wanted us to have a better life than he had, but he had lived enough to understand that nobody is entitled to anything in this world.

'Don't try to be like somebody else,' he'd tell me. 'Don't try to live somebody else's life. It's your life. Don't let other people try to change you. If you want something or if you want to do something, you have to make the change yourself. You make the difference. You're the only person who can do that.'

Whenever we were talking about work or money, he would point to my uncles in Kurdistan. They had built a good life for themselves when they went back after the war, but they had worked hard for it.

'Look at my brothers. They work on a farm during the day, and they drive taxis in the evening, and that's why they don't have mortgages. If you want to buy a house, Allah isn't going to hand you the money. The government isn't going to hand you the money. If that's what you want, you have to work hard for it. If you have to work two jobs, work two jobs.'

My dad wasn't worried about his own life in Ireland. His only concern was for me and my brothers and sisters, and our future here. He wanted to make sure all eleven of us got set up, got into school, learned English, got on the right track, got good jobs, and were happy. That was how he spent his time and energy. We were his number one priority.

I loved that hurling, my passion, could be a bit of an outlet for him too. I could see that he got great enjoyment out of coming to the games. Like myself, he had to get to grips with the rules at first, but once he could follow the game, he had a real appreciation for how it's played and the skill of it. I didn't need a lift to most matches, but I knew that if I asked him, he'd be only too delighted to bring me. I hated to think of him hanging around the house when he could have been out getting a bit of fresh air and watching me. The post-match analysis sessions in the car on the way home were a small price to pay.

Everyone on the team got to know him. He wouldn't go up to a match without bringing his little notebook and pen with him. He would stand there watching, taking a note of every score as it went over. If there was any uncertainty, or if the lads on the line needed an update, they knew that they could rely on him in his role as unofficial scorekeeper.

Sometimes the two of us would go up to the club together to watch a match that I wasn't playing in, the senior footballers or another team. One thing my dad always noticed was when someone didn't fully commit to a tackle or pulled out at the last minute, when they were afraid to get stuck in or worried that they might get hurt. I know he noticed it in hurling too, spotting the lads who wouldn't even put their hurl in, never mind their hand, to try to win some dirty ball. 'It's a tough man's game,' he'd say. 'It's a tough man's game.' But I never thought I'd see the day when he would be the one out there getting stuck in on the pitch.

I don't remember exactly when this happened; I was still young enough, maybe late teens or early twenties, but I was already on the Thomas Davis senior hurling panel. We had a game against Ballyboden St Enda's, one of our big local rivals, the kind of game that you tog out for knowing that you're not going to get an inch. I didn't even get that much from my marker that day.

There was the usual pulling and dragging, me ducking and diving to try to get into a yard of space and get on the ball, him making sure that he had his hurl in one hand and a handful of my jersey in the other at all times. Before I could try to get away from him again, he grabbed me around the neck and pulled me into a headlock. I was trying to push him off me but he had me held tight, and he wasn't letting me go. I was shouting, hoping that I'd get the referee's attention or, if not, your man might panic and let me go before he got sent off. I could hear the management and the subs on the sideline roaring too as soon as they spotted what was happening. But the ball was away down the other end of the pitch, and the referee was gone with it, so we could shout and roar all we wanted; nobody was coming to help me.

It was only when my dad caught hold of him that this fella finally let go of me. I didn't even realise what was happening because at that stage, all hell was breaking loose and my dad was right there in the thick of it. He had run onto the pitch to drag the guy off me, and when he did everyone piled in behind him, the Ballyboden lads rushing to jump in for their team-mate and the Thomas Davis lads arriving in to back up me and my dad. Eventually the referee arrived – far too late to help me, thanks – and managed to get everybody separated and calm things down. My dad was told to get off the pitch and get back to the sideline, and the rest of us got back to hurling.

My dad never had time for fools or for messing, in any walk of life, but even though he was a quiet man, I never mistook that quietness for weakness. I always knew he was a hardy man, very old school, and if he felt he needed to fight, then there was going to be a fight, and there was only going to be one winner.

I found him after the game. 'You can't be running onto the pitch like that,' I told him, but he just looked at me and shook his head. He didn't need to say anything because the look said it all:

I'll do it again if I have to.

ROBBED

The year 2010 should have been our year in Thomas Davis. The memories of that season should be some of the happiest of my career, be it with club or county. Instead, any time I think about it, I just get angry. I'm still not over it.

We had a really good season. Actually, we had a great season. Shane Plowman was the senior hurling manager, and when he looked at everyone available to him – the experienced lads who had been doing it at senior level for a long time, and the good young lads who were just starting to push on from underage – he knew that he had the right mix of players to put together a strong, balanced panel. I was only nineteen but in Shane's eyes, if you were good enough to play, you were old enough to play. I got plenty of opportunities.

The ambition was to win a county title, but the Dublin intermediate championship is fiercely competitive, and

Thomas Davis know better than most that silverware of any kind is brutally hard to come by. At that time, our club had won four Dublin senior titles in over one hundred and twenty years of existence. Three of them were in football, an incredible three-in-a-row in the late 1980s and early 1990s; the sole senior hurling title was all the way back before the First World War – in 1913.

We worked hard in training all season, and it showed in our performances. When the intermediate championship rolled around, we looked strong, and we qualified out of our group. The club had got to the intermediate final a few years earlier, in 2006, and lost, and we didn't need Shane or any of the players who had been on that team to remind us that seasons like this don't come around every year. We had an opportunity here, and we couldn't afford to let it slip through our fingers. We played Commercials from Rathcoole in the semi-final, and came from six points down at half time to win by a point. We were into the county final, and word quickly came through from the other semi-final: Kevin's had beaten Kilmacud Crokes. We would have a week to prepare for them; the final was scheduled for the following Saturday. Parnell Park was calling our name.

In all of the controversy that followed the final, one thing that I couldn't get away from was that it was all so avoidable. If only we could have held on for just another few moments and closed the game out, nothing else would have mattered.

We started well in the first half against Kevin's. I was in at wing-forward and between the six of us, we were carving out chances and taking our scores, enough of them anyway. But it was a real back-and-forth; every time they landed a punch and tried to build on their momentum, we had an answer. It was the same story during our good spells; we were able to hold them at arm's length once or twice, but never any more than that.

We scored two goals in the first half and went in at half time four points up, 2-6 to 1-5, and then finally managed to take control in the second half. We were winning by six at one stage but Kevin's dug in and kept doing enough to keep themselves alive. They were running out of time, though. Points were no good to them. All we needed to do was to keep them out, to stop them from scoring goals for the final few minutes and the game would be over. Time was practically up when they got the goal that they were chasing, one last flash of hope. And then they got another, and another.

When something like that happens, it happens so quickly that it's hard to fully take it in. We had one hand on the championship but now we were the ones left like ghosts on the pitch as they celebrated and ran up the steps to lift the cup. It should have been us but it wasn't. We lost the game by five points, 4-8 to 2-9.

Our heads were spinning, and I'm not sure who was the first person on our side to realise that something wasn't quite right, or who was the first to ask the question. We knew two of the subs that they had brought off the bench. There was a strong suspicion that they shouldn't have been in the squad, never mind on the pitch, because they hadn't been properly registered to play.

What could we do? We had such high hopes for the season, we had poured everything into it, and now it was over and we had nothing to show for it except this sucker-punch of a defeat. We did the only thing we could do. We went on the beer.

The next day, a group of us headed out to Flannery's pub on Camden Street. The Kevin's lads were there too, their party still going strong. All we could do was watch as they kept topping up the cup with beer and passing it around so that they could take turns drinking out of it. I took a drink out of the cup and turned back to my team-mates.

'This is our cup,' I told them. I could see the confused look on the faces of the Kevin's lads, wondering what I was up to.

'This cup will be back in Tallaght soon, just wait and see,' I said. 'You knew those two boys shouldn't have been playing.'

'No, no, no. You don't know what you're talking about.'

'I'm telling you,' I insisted. 'This is our cup.'

And I was right. The club lodged an appeal over the result to the Dublin County Board, and it was upheld. The two players were found to be ineligible – they should never have played. The result of the final was overturned, and Kevin's forfeited the game and the championship. A couple of days later, John Costello, the CEO of the Dublin County Board, arrived at our clubhouse with the cup. Now it was our turn to fill it with beer and pass it around and take the photos.

'You see, I told you,' I reminded the lads, but I didn't feel happy. None of us did. We were the Dublin intermediate hurling champions, but it was by default. It was the most hollow victory.

We couldn't celebrate it. I didn't even feel sick. I just felt empty, absolutely drained. We had put in a full year of work and training and matches, made commitments, made sacrifices, to try to do something special as a group. The feeling of achieving that together, for our club, of hearing the final whistle and knowing that every drill, every yard run in training, had all been worth it in the end – we never got to share that moment. We never had that feeling. It was all taken away from us by a team who had played ineligible players. What was the point of it all? Why had we even bothered if this was how it was going to turn out? It just wasn't right.

We had our few drinks that night and then we got back to training. Our season wasn't over after all. It should have been an honour for us to go out and represent our club and our county in the Leinster junior championship, but in the circumstances, it didn't feel like that. We tried to get our heads right before we played Drumcullen of Offaly in the first round but everything felt very flat to me that week. It wasn't anyone's fault. We weren't really interested. We just felt that we shouldn't be there.

It showed on the pitch. Drumcullen hammered us and quickly put us out of our misery. I've never been so glad to see the back of a season.

LEITRIM CALLING

'So, will you give us one year?' Martin Cunniffe asked me. 'Will you come down and give us one year?'

In the years after we moved to Dublin, I never lost touch with my friends in Leitrim. When I transferred to Thomas Davis and was no longer playing for St Mary's and Carrick, the bus journeys down and back became less frequent, but they never stopped. If I had a free weekend with no matches and no work, I'd head down for a night to catch up with everyone. There was always a match to go to and a pint to drink afterwards; there still is.

If I stayed with the Singletons, myself and Barry would stroll around to the club or jump in the car and head off to watch whatever match Darragh was playing in. It's twenty years now since I left Leitrim, but the St Mary's and Carrick teams still look the same. So many of the lads I made friends with as an eleven- or twelve-year-old are still there and still going strong – which makes us the auld fellas now, I guess. When they introduce me to the younger players, it's a brother of someone I played with, or a cousin of someone I know. The same handful of families are still the backbone of the clubs after all these years.

The Cunniffes are one of those families. Clement is the greatest hurler Leitrim ever produced, as well as being the man who first put a hurl in my hand. His mam, Dolores, and his sister Miriam have dedicated so much of their lives to hurling in Carrick and Leitrim down through the years. And then there's his dad, Martin. Martin is originally from Galway. He moved to Carrick in the seventies because of his work in the guards, and in one capacity or another, he's been involved in Carrick hurling and in Leitrim GAA pretty much ever since. He hurled for the club, he hurled for the county, he coached generation after generation of young players and taught them to love the game, and he did whatever administrative jobs were needed to keep the whole show on the road.

When Martin took over as Leitrim manager in 2011, his number one priority was to keep hurling in the county alive. That was a big enough challenge by itself, and by no means a foregone conclusion, so anything more than that would be an incredible bonus. Martin knew Leitrim hurling inside out, so he knew the size of the task. He had been there as part of Kevin Glancy's backroom team in 2010 in what had been

Kevin's final year as manager. There were thirty-five counties in the National Hurling League that season when you include London, Fingal and South Down; Leitrim won just one game and finished second from bottom in Division 4. It was the same in Martin's first year, with only Cavan having a worse league campaign than them that spring. The performances and the results don't lie. That was their level: the thirty-fourth best team out of thirty-five.

Counties at Leitrim's level don't even enter the main All-Ireland senior hurling championship, the Liam MacCarthy Cup. There would be no point in pitching them against Kilkenny or Cork or Tipperary or any of the other heavyweight counties; they simply wouldn't stand a chance. There has been a 'B' Championship for the weaker counties since the 1970s, but starting in 2005, the GAA began to restructure the competition into a series of lower tiers so that every county could play in a championship that they could genuinely aspire to win.

In 2009 they introduced the Lory Meagher Cup, which was the fourth tier at the time, and is now the fifth. That was where Leitrim played. If the league had been a struggle for Leitrim in 2010, there was a lot more promise in their championship performances. They made it to the Lory Meagher semi-finals before losing to Longford in what was Kevin's final game before he handed over the reins.

It was a world away from 82,000-capacity crowds in Croke Park in the summer, but that was the level that

Leitrim badly wanted to be competitive at. Martin was a firm believer that if you're stuck down at the bottom, the only way is up. Not everybody felt the same way, though, and there was talk around the place in the summer of 2011 that Leitrim should consider pulling out of the National Hurling League entirely and focus instead on improving the underage set-up. That was how bad things had become. But Martin and everyone who loved Leitrim hurling wouldn't hear of it. It was a crucial argument to win; Cavan did withdraw, promising that they would be back again in a couple of seasons, but they didn't field a senior hurling team again for the next six years.

That was the shape of Leitrim hurling as I stood on the line in Carrick that day, watching a club game, chatting away to Martin and Kevin. They were asking me about Dublin, about the club, about how I was getting on, and then Martin cut to the chase.

'Will you come down so? Just give it a go for a year.'

I knew by Martin that he was deadly serious, that this was a genuine request. I'd have to think about it. I was already playing intermediate football with Thomas Davis, as well as hurling, and going in with Leitrim on top of that would be a huge commitment. At the same time, I knew I needed something fresh. I was still stung by everything that had happened in the 2010 championship, and I had lost a little bit of interest because of it; not much, but enough. It would be good to try something new.

'How would I even get down?' I asked him. 'Sure I don't drive, I don't have a car.'

Once I didn't say no straight away, Martin knew that he had me on the hook. 'Oh there's plenty of cars coming from Dublin, there'll be no problems with that. We'll feed you too, we'll give you the bacon and cabbage,' he laughed. 'What else do you want?'

Any manager of a weaker county, whether it's in football or hurling, has an incredibly tough job. Expectations are higher in the top counties, of course, but those teams also get the support that they need to succeed. People often say that money isn't going to puck the ball over the bar for you, and that's true – but what they forget is that if you don't even have enough money to buy the balls in the first place, you're not going to get very far.

In theory, it should cost roughly the same amount of money every week to run the Leitrim senior hurling team as it does any other inter-county team – in reality, we spend less because we're scrimping and saving everywhere we can, because we still have to find a way to balance the books without a big sponsor that will write us a multi-million-euro cheque for a five-year deal. We don't have the same facilities either. We're lucky to have a brilliant Centre of Excellence now, but that has only been officially open since 2019, and there's a shortage of AstroTurf pitches in the county, which makes organising training sessions a nightmare at certain times of the year.

And yet Martin, like any other manager of a weaker county, still had to find a way to prepare the team and get us playing to the best of our ability and send us out there to compete. He didn't have a massive pool of players to choose from. There were only four senior hurling clubs at that time: Carrick, Manorhamilton, Ballinamore and Gortletteragh. A lot of those squads were made up of dual players who didn't want to give up football to dedicate themselves to hurling. When all was said and done, Martin probably had about forty players to pick from in the entire county; my club manager at Thomas Davis had more options than that.

When I first went in ahead of the 2012 season, Martin and his management team, Brían Carroll and Paddy O'Connor, couldn't even be sure of what they had to work with. Ireland was still reeling from the recession and Leitrim had been hit as hard as anywhere in the country, if not harder. One night at a training session, we had thirty players togged out; within a few weeks, three or four of them were going to Australia. Martin understood the importance of finding a way to work with the players he did have. Someone might come to him and say, 'I won't make it tomorrow evening. I'll have to work,' and Martin understood.

'Oh jaysus, don't worry,' he'd reassure them. 'Go to work. Hurling is only a hobby.'

My dad drove me down to my very first training session, and sat outside the sports hall in the car and waited until we were done so that he could drive me back home again afterwards. Brían took training that night for a strength and conditioning session, and I quickly realised that inter-county hurling – no matter what level it's at – is a completely different beast from the club game. There's a different intensity to it, a different physicality, and Brían wanted to make sure that we could last the pace.

He put us through the mill that night until everybody was absolutely shattered. I could see the lads getting annoyed that the session was too tough – 'What are we doing inside in a sports hall? We should be outside hurling' – but Brían was ahead of his time. He saw which way the game was evolving, and he knew that our skills and our tactics wouldn't matter in the slightest if we weren't fit enough to keep running in the last ten minutes.

Martin threw me straight in for my debut in the first league game of the season, away to Longford, and I scored a couple of points in a twelve-point win. Longford were in a bad way at the time, and that scoreline was as much a reflection on them as it was on us, as we quickly found out when we went out to play Fermanagh the following week. They beat us by thirty-three points, 6-27 to 2-6.

That left us in no doubt about where we stood. Martin's message was the same as it would be over the years: if that's where we're at, if that's the starting point, let's improve from there, let's get closer. Yes, we lost by thirty-three points. Let's make sure that it's only thirty-two the next day.

We got a chance to put that to the test before the summer was out. When we came up against Fermanagh again in the semi-finals of the Lory Meagher, we were far more competitive. We still lost the game, but this time it was only by seven points. It was a small step, but at least it was a step in the right direction.

KURDISH BLOOD

A friend of mine owns his own business in Dublin. Sometimes, when he is chatting to a customer, they will ask about his life.

'My family are Kurdish. We are from Kurdistan originally,' he explains, which can lead to a puzzled look and another question.

'Where's Kurdistan?'

He once drew a little map to show a customer, sketching in borders through the different parts of Iraq, Iran, Turkey and Syria. 'That's Kurdistan,' he explained. 'That's where my family comes from.'

Every Kurdish person feels the same: if we don't talk about our politics, if we don't celebrate our culture, if we don't keep Kurdistan alive in our hearts and in our words, nobody else will.

All Kurds are political. When Kurdish people meet

170

up or visit each other's homes, we talk about politics; it's how we were brought up. Even though we are united by our love for our country and our dream of having a home of our own, we are divided in so many ways. Every Kurdish area has its own ideology; every little village is like its own little country; every side feels that their way is the right way, the best way. There are multiple different political parties in each Kurdish region, and they all have their own agenda. Post-Saddam, the power-sharing agreement in Iraq effectively guarantees that the president of the country is a Kurd; when I'm out with friends, they can't even agree on who it should be, whether it should belong to the PDK or PUK, the Barzanis or the Talabanis. Sometimes, with so many differences, it becomes very difficult to see how there could ever be a united Kurdistan.

It is our culture that brings us together. All Kurdish people love two things: music and dancing. For a long time, Kurdish music was deeply political. The most famous musicians, like Şivan Perwer, wrote songs and stories about the Kurdish struggle for freedom. They celebrated the *peshmerga*, the men and women who had fought and died for our country. A lot of newer music isn't as openly political. Instead, it's based on older, traditional Kurdish songs, which are being reimagined and modernised by young musicians.

I listen to Kurdish music all the time; I love it. Two of

my brothers, Mokhtar and Jamal, have businesses that promote Kurdish music online. They keep an eye out for talented singers, people who have a great voice but might not necessarily be that well known, and get them to record clips that they can share online. They don't do it to make money. They do it for the love of it.

There are so many more Kurds living in Ireland now than when we first arrived, but it is hard for everyone to stay connected. We come together to celebrate Newroz, the Kurdish new year, every March. For our family back home in Kermanshah, the Newroz celebrations are a massive party that might last for two or three weeks. A few of my brothers try to visit at that time of year so that they can celebrate with our relatives. In the videos they send back, there seem to be thousands of people listening to music and dancing. Here, the celebrations only last for a day or two at most. Either we will visit one of the Kurdish families we are close to, or they will come to visit us, and we'll sit down and share a meal together: maybe some lamb chops with Kurdish dolma, which are stuffed vegetables, and rice.

A couple of times a year, we might organise a cultural event to bring people together. For Newroz one year, one of the most famous Kurdish singers, Aziz Waisi, came to Dublin to perform. We booked a room in a hotel, everybody got dressed up in their best Kurdish clothes, and we had a party with lots of music and dancing.

Halparke is our traditional Kurdish dance. It's a little bit like Irish set dancing: everybody joins hands and forms a line to dance side by side. There are some imams and devout Muslims who disapprove of it because it is *haram*, forbidden by the Quran, and there are the older men who sit off to the side, refusing to dance, because they want to be seen as serious and respectable. I'm always watching to see how long they can hold out for. They see everybody else dancing and having fun, or a woman will invite them to come and join the dance:

'Why are you sitting down? Come up and dance.'

'Ah no, I'm too old for that, I couldn't with my back.'

'Ah, come on.'

'Oh, okay, I'll just give it one dance and see.'

They're only waiting to be asked so that they have a reason to join in. Once they're up there, there's no stopping them.

When we dress up for a celebration like that, Kurdish women will wear their gold. It's a very traditional part of Kurdish culture: in Ireland, a man might buy a diamond engagement ring to propose; in Kurdish culture, he buys gold. It's seen as proof that he will be able to provide for his future wife and family, but it's also a guarantee that he is serious about the marriage. The man has to spend at least a couple of thousand euro, which is a few months' salary or more for a lot of people in Iran. An imam might even ask for details – 'Did you buy the gold? How much did it cost?' – so that he can take note of the value when he's filling out the marriage paperwork. If the marriage ends in divorce, the woman will keep it all.

There are other parts of Kurdish culture which have started to fade away. Traditional Kurdish tattoos, or *deq*, were very common among my parents' generation. Nearly every Kurdish person of that age has tattoos on their hands or running up along their arms, and a lot of women would have them on their neck and their face as well. Whether it's a moon or a star or another pattern or drawing, they all have their own little histories.

When we were in Al-Tash camp, it was so normal for people to have tattoos that nobody would even comment on them, but time has moved on and the tradition is dying out. When I got my first tattoo, my whole family went mad. I got it on my right forearm, a design of a compass and a flower.

'We're trying to get rid of tattoos and you're going and putting tattoos on you,' my mam said when she first saw it. 'You look stupid, you will regret that,' my brothers and sisters warned, but I don't regret it at all. I'm really happy that I got it done.

Throughout history, the oppressors have always believed that if you can stop a culture, you can stop a people. But the Kurdish people will never give in. That's why, even after twenty years in Ireland, my heritage and these customs and traditions are still so important to me

– they're important to every Kurd. They will always be a part of who I am. My heart belongs to Ireland now, but my blood will for ever be Kurdish.

GOING HOME

My dad had a few old video tapes that he loved.
He must have watched them nearly every
week.

To anybody else, they would have been worthless,
videos of fields and farms in the Kurdish mountains that
his brothers had sent him. There was nothing special about
them. They were just camcorder footage of village life,
normal people going about their everyday business, tilling
their land and tending to their crops and animals. That's
what made them so special to him.

After my family fled Zahaw in 1980, it would be thirty
years before they even returned to visit the wider family.
Until that time came, these videos were the only thing that
allowed my dad to go home. They were his only way to see
the place he had grown up in, the fields he had played in as
a child. It was a little bit different than he remembered it – it

had been rebuilt after the Iran–Iraq war – but at least he knew he hadn't imagined it. It did exist, out there in the real world, in somewhere other than his heart. Every time he watched the videos it was a chance to catch up with the people he loved, people he hadn't been able to hug in a very long time. He could see their faces again, see that they were well, that they were living life as it had always been before. It didn't matter how many times he watched those tapes. They made him so happy.

My dad loved Ireland. He loved this country for what it had done for us, the gift that it had so generously given our family. His was a gratitude that could never be fully expressed, for a debt that it was impossible to repay. Ireland was his home now, but Kurdistan was his home too. It was possible for those two things to be true at the same time. It didn't have to be one place or the other; it couldn't be.

It was his dream to go back to Kurdistan some day. My parents always hoped that they would have that chance when we were all grown up and finished in school. They never planned to leave Ireland completely – that wasn't what they wanted either – but they wanted to spend time in Kurdistan, more than just a few weeks for a visit. If they could figure out a way that would allow them to spend six months there and six months here, that would have been perfect.

In 2010, my parents went back to Zahaw for the first time since the Iran–Iraq war, and for the first time in nearly twenty years, my dad saw his parents. When they separated

177

in the aftermath of the Gulf War and my grandparents left Al-Tash camp to try to return home to Kurdistan, nobody knew what the future held. They all understood the dangers involved, that there was no guarantee that my grandparents and my uncles could even get home safely, that sneaking back over the border was a life-or-death risk. It was a risk that they felt they had to take. They never lost hope that peace would come again, that they would have a better life, and that better life would be back home in Zahaw, where they belonged. When my family said their impossible goodbyes that day, they could never have imagined that they would spend so much of their lives apart.

My dad missed his parents every day. War had cost him so much of his life with them and even as we all built our safe and happy futures, both here and there, he was still carrying that cost. Ireland had given so much of his life back to him, but it could never give him one of the things that mattered most, or the time that had been lost over the years. Every day that passed was a missed opportunity, another day when they could have been together again instead of 3,000 miles apart. As he got older, his parents did too, and his need to go back to Kurdistan became even more urgent.

My parents had done so much for us, and now it was our turn to do something for them. My brothers and sisters and I saved until we had enough money put aside to book their flights for them. Before they left, we gave them the rest of the money we had saved. It was enough to cover anything that they might need while they were there and last them until they came home again. They had waited so long for this visit that we wanted to make sure that they could enjoy themselves without worrying. It was lovely to be able to take care of them in that way, but no matter what you do for your parents, you always feel that it isn't enough, that you could have and should have done more.

The next time my parents visited Kurdistan was in 2013. My grandparents had built a house for our family beside all my dad's brothers' houses, for us to use whenever we visited, but my parents preferred to stay with them in their house. Any time they could spend together was special, and it didn't make sense to go home to a different house in the evening, even if it was only a couple of hundred yards down the hill. They were there for a month on that occasion. I called them every couple of days to see how they were getting on. I knew when they were due to come back to Ireland. I'd see them both again soon.

I'd been out with my friends the night my dad died. We'd had a brilliant night, out until all hours enjoying ourselves and catching up. I wasn't long home, and only just after getting into bed, when my phone rang. It was still early, far too early for phone calls. I saw my brother Mokhtar's name flash up on the screen. When I answered, he told me the bad news.

Nothing can prepare you for that conversation. In one moment, life is as unremarkable as you could ask for, fast asleep in bed after a great night out. In the next, it has changed for ever. The permanent reassuring presence of my dad was the one thing that I could be certain about in the chaos of my childhood. Whatever the problem was, he knew how to tackle it, because we had come through worse situations before. He was always there for me, for all of us, until he wasn't. That's the hardest part to come to terms with: when a loved one is stolen away from you without warning, without a proper chance to say goodbye.

My dad died on the aeroplane, on my parents' journey from Kurdistan back to Ireland. Their flight was mid-air on the way to Istanbul when he had a heart attack. The pilot turned the plane around and made an emergency landing in Tehran, but it was too late. My dad's remains were brought home to Kurdistan. He is buried in Zahaw, right next to the family farm.

ABOUT DAD

When a loved one passes away, there is some consolation if they have lived a long and full life into old age, but my dad was only fifty-seven when he died. In a lot of ways, it felt like his life was only just getting started. After all the suffering he and my mam had been through together, they had reached a point where they were no longer living in a state of permanent trauma. Things had settled down. In the eleven years he spent in Ireland, life had become normal. For the first time, they were allowing themselves to think about the future, to make plans. They could never get back the years that war had stolen from them, but they could make the most of the ones that they still had ahead of them. They didn't want to travel the world. They didn't want anything other than a simple life that they could share in peace with their family. When he finally got that, my dad didn't realise how little time he would have to enjoy it. None of us did.

I didn't go to my dad's funeral. I couldn't do it. I was too upset. My mam had brought his remains back home to Zahaw so that he could be buried in Kurdistan, in the little village that he spent most of his life trying to get back to. My mam stayed there for a month afterwards and two of my brothers, Raoof and Bakhtiar, flew out to join her for the funeral. The rest of us decided to stay at home. I would have found it too hard.

I always knew my dad was a popular man, but I saw just how popular he was in the weeks after he died. Our funeral for him in Ireland lasted for nearly a month. There wasn't a day that went past without a knock on the door of our house in Old Bawn, and every time we opened it, there was a familiar face. Family and friends flew in from Sweden, Norway and England. Jawhar Ahmadi, my dad's great friend from when we lived in Al-Tash camp, and his wife came all the way from Canada to be with us in person. They had been resettled in Alberta, and as soon as they heard the news, they went straight to the airport to jump on a flight. We didn't even know that they were coming until they arrived at the house. They didn't have to do it, they could have just made a phone call, but it meant so much to us that they did. That connection from our time in Al-Tash camp was still there. People never forgot what they had come through together. They were always there for each other.

They were difficult days, but as people came and sat down with us and shared their stories and their memories, some happy and some sad, it gave us all a chance to remember my dad as he was. It wasn't just our family who were grieving. We knew that we weren't alone, that we all shared the same loss. So many people spoke so highly of him, and about what he meant to them, that there was no doubt that he had lived a good life.

There's a video that was taken of my parents during one of their trips to Kurdistan. When they landed in the airport, there were dozens of people waiting there to welcome him home. It's such comforting footage, watching my dad in the middle as everybody came to greet him with hugs and kisses, and then later, another stream of people visiting the house when they arrived back to the village. We sometimes watch those old tapes of my dad, but it's very emotional. I still find them almost too difficult to watch, seeing him there but knowing that he is gone.

I'll always think of him as a very easy-going man, but life had hardened him too, and I know that he could be tough when he needed to be. He hated fighting and rows and arguments, conflict of any kind. He had seen so much of it in his life, and seen how pointless and destructive it all ultimately was. 'One hour's talk with a dictator is better than twenty years of war,' I remember him saying to me once; he knew that it is the innocent people who suffer the most in war.

That was his attitude in every walk of life, so he never fell out with anybody. 'Never argue when you're out,' he always reminded me. 'It doesn't matter, just walk away.' I've never thrown a dig in my life. If I do have an argument, it'd be forgotten about by the next day. My dad taught me never to hold a grudge, to forgive and forget, to shake hands and move on. Whatever happened yesterday was yesterday; today is another day.

He was like my grandfather, very respected, and if he spoke, people listened. He was also very diplomatic. If there was a row in the community, a disagreement between families or a fight at a football match or whatever it might be, Kurdish people never wanted to involve the police. Instead, they would come to our house: 'Your house was like the courtroom,' someone said to me once. Both sides would sit down with my dad and explain what had happened, and he would listen to all the different arguments and perspectives, and when he had figured out what they needed to do, he'd give them his advice on how to make it right again.

I was driving through Tallaght one day when I spotted a Kurdish man around my dad's age walking in the village. I didn't really know the man but I pulled over to offer him a lift, and he jumped into the car beside me. We had a good chat as we drove, and I told him that I was Safar Moradi's son.

'There were only two Kurdish gentlemen in Ireland,' he said when he knew who I was. 'There were only two Kurdish

men that you could talk to, and your dad was one of them.'
This was a good few years after my dad had died. It was
lovely for me to hear how fondly he was remembered in the
community.

My dad was never interested in money. If he had it, he'd
find somebody who was worse off than he was and try to
help them. My mam is the very same. It wouldn't bother her
to have nothing; she has never worried about what she
doesn't have. 'Ah, it's only paper,' she'd say. The only thing
my dad cared about was that we grew up safe and happy,
that we had our jobs and worked hard and cherished the
time that we spent with our family and friends. That was all
he ever wanted for us in life. That was all he ever wanted for
himself.

My dad was the biggest influence on my life. I see all the
best parts of myself in him. I miss him every day.

ON THE
ROAD AGAIN

I'm sure I could nearly list the road signs off by heart if I tried. If there was a quiz question about the towns and villages at every motorway junction between Tallaght and Leitrim, you'd want me on your team. Nobody ever sees the hours that you spend in the car, back and forth and back and forth. I never minded going to training; it was the driving that I hated.

We trained twice a week with Leitrim, starting at eight o'clock most evenings. If I wasn't finished work and in the car by five o'clock at the absolute latest, I had no chance of being there on time. Even at that, it was always a rush. The drive takes about an hour and forty-five minutes at the best of times, longer again if you're taking a detour to pick up a team-mate for a bit of company, and at that time of evening, you can be guaranteed at least another hour spent in traffic looking at the reg plate of the car sitting in front of you. I'd be one of the last to pull into the car park, with barely enough time to tie the laces on my boots and get properly stretched. If we were finished by ten o'clock and I was back in the car on the road home a few minutes later, I was lucky. Even at that, it would still be well after midnight by the time I crawled into bed, my alarm set for work the following morning.

Doing that commute once a week is bad enough; doing it twice is guaranteed to leave you shattered. Somewhere in the middle of all of that driving, there was a training session too; it wasn't exactly a gentle evening jog. The weekends weren't much better. If we were playing at home, it was another four-hour round trip with a game sandwiched in the middle. If we had an away game, or had a challenge match lined up somewhere else in the country, it could easily be more than that again. By the time I got home, the day would be gone.

There were plenty of nights when we'd meet halfway for training, somewhere in the Midlands, not out of convenience but because it was the only place where we could find a pitch. In the winter and spring, you can't have an evening training session without floodlights, and the floodlit pitches in Leitrim were regularly booked up for football. Martin would be on the phone to Paddy O'Connor, one of his selectors, and have him ringing around clubs in Westmeath or Offaly to see if they would let us use a pitch for an hour or two. Paddy would leave no stone unturned but in the end, after a string of nos, he might have to settle for half a pitch somewhere, just to make sure that we had somewhere to go. We didn't have much choice.

People often ask about the sacrifices that you have to make as an inter-county hurler, the dedication that's involved. You describe your routine and they struggle to believe that's the reality for an amateur sport. That is what it takes – but I wouldn't do it if I didn't love it.

There were Saturdays when my brother Hoshar would drive me down to a match in Leitrim in plenty of time to get togged out for a twelve o'clock throw-in. I'd play the full seventy minutes, get driven back up to Dublin, and then play another full game with Thomas Davis that evening at seven o'clock. On a good day, I'd manage to get a bit of sleep in the car between matches. I didn't advertise the fact that I was doing it. I didn't really expect anyone to care.

At the height of it, between training and matches, I must have been hurling five or six days out of seven every week. I enjoyed it, even though I was barely getting a proper night's sleep and I was always wrecked, but part of it was down to me trying to keep everyone happy. Even when Leitrim's season was in full swing, I tried not to miss club training. When it comes to the club, I would never describe myself as a hurling man or a football man; I'm a Thomas Davis man. I played with the intermediate footballers for a while as well, and I'd get a call sometimes from someone involved with them or with the juniors: they were short a few players, a load of lads were injured, and they were worried that they wouldn't have enough to field a team. If I could be the difference between forfeiting the match or not, I never wanted to be the one to let them down.

I trained hard because I knew that anything less wouldn't be good enough. I love the skill of hurling; there's nothing like it in the world. But there's only one way to keep your touch sharp, to keep your eye in, and that's through practice. The best hurlers, the masters, are the ones who are working on their game every single week. If you haven't picked up a hurl for a few weeks, it's obvious. You're way off the pace. You're miles behind. As a sport, it demands complete dedication, nothing less.

When I started out hurling, I played in midfield, but I've been a forward for most of my career. I'm average height – I'm 5'10", maybe 5'11" if I flick my fringe up – but if there's a man mountain of a full back towering over me, I probably seem smaller than I am. I'm sure that's how I ended up playing as a corner-forward. High balls were never my strength. I was always better at getting the ball off the ground into my hand, getting my head up and using the ball, or getting stuck into a crowd of three or four, battling for a dirty ball, and coming away with it.

When you're a forward, everybody sees you; there's nowhere to hide. People watching on the sideline, in the stands or on TV might miss little details all over the pitch but they always see the shots and they always count the wides. That's the bottom line. Of course some wides are caused by bad decisions: the shot was never on; it should have been a pass instead. Even on my bad days, I preferred to look at the positives. Before you can hit a wide, you have to win a ball, get into space and get your shot away, so you're doing something right. Other forwards might not even be getting on the ball, but it rarely gets noticed. If you hit a few wides, that's the only thing that people see. All the other good things you did – the possession you won, the frees you earned, the scores you set up, your hooks, blocks and tackles – are forgotten.

I like to think that I thrived on that pressure. I tried to hang around in the right areas, anticipating what was going to happen next, making sure that I would be the first to react. It worked for me. It was always worth a couple of goals every season.

We took some decent hidings in my first couple of seasons with Leitrim. That day when Fermanagh beat us by thirty-three points was the worst, thankfully, and that same season, Tyrone beat us by twenty-five points in the opening round of the Lory Meagher before we went on to make it to the semi-finals. There were a few more double-digit defeats as well. Lads at home in Thomas Davis would be looking at the amount of driving and training I was doing, and then looking up our results at the weekend to see how we had got on. There'd be a bit of slagging – 'Ah Jesus, what are you at down there?' – but I never minded that. What I didn't like was when people I didn't know would ask, 'Sure is there even hurling down in Leitrim?', chuckling away as if it was the funniest thought anyone ever had. It was so dismissive of the efforts we were putting in, and more than that, it was hugely disrespectful to Martin and Kevin and Paddy and everyone else who had worked so hard for so long to keep the game alive.

Better days were on the way, though, and the 2014 league campaign was the start of it. We lost our opening match against Tyrone, although this time there was only four points in it, and then we beat Sligo the next day out. Going into the final round of matches, we knew that all we needed was a draw at home to Warwickshire to send us through to the Division 3B league final. They had won the Lory Meagher the previous season; getting something from the game would be no small task.

Games against either Warwickshire or Lancashire – two of the GAA's Exile 'counties' in Britain – were our worst nightmare because we never knew what to expect. It was easy to get a read on all our other opponents because the vast majority of their squad stayed the same from year to year, but it felt like Warwickshire and Lancashire had a few aces up their sleeve every season. If any decent hurler moved over to England for work or for personal reasons, and they wanted to keep playing, they would put through a transfer to play for one team or the other. It made them incredibly unpredictable to play against, which I didn't like. We could never be confident about how we matched up against them because we never knew what new faces they would have. Even if we were going well, there was a fear that we could be ambushed. This time, we got the job done: we were five points up with five minutes to play but by the end, we were praying for the whistle. We won 0-15 to 1-11.

Once we were into the league final, we set our sights on winning it, but we had already taken a major step forward just by getting there. It had been twenty-seven years since Leitrim's hurlers had played in the 1987 Division 4 league final. Martin was in the starting fifteen that day; I hadn't even been born.

Leitrim had lost against Tyrone that day, and by chance, the same county was waiting for us again in the final. By any neutral assessment, Tyrone were the clear favourites. They had been playing in Division 3A for the previous two seasons and, despite their relegation back to 3B, they were used to hurling at a slightly higher level than us, with all of the advantages that brought. Our recent record against them looked very one-sided. None of that bothered us. If the prospect of us winning was being billed as a shock or an upset, we didn't see it that way. We gave ourselves every chance that day – we were five points up in the early part of the second half – but Tyrone pegged us back and then beat us with the last puck of the game, a long-range free from their captain and star man Damian Casey. It finished 0-13 to 1-9. Tyrone were the league champions; they were promoted back to Division 3A; and we left Markievicz Park empty-handed, with nothing to show except for a glimmer of reassurance that we were finally on the right track.

EXCEPT IRAN

I sat down and started to write a letter to the Department of Justice, explaining what I needed. I asked them for their help so that I could do something that I had wanted to do for a long time. I wanted to see my grandparents and my uncles and cousins. I wanted to see the village where my parents had grown up, this beautiful place that I had heard about for all my life. I wanted to finally go to Kurdistan.

I didn't have a passport. All I had was the travel document that the Irish government had issued to me when we first arrived in the country. It was so precious. It gave me the freedom to go anywhere, to travel to any country I liked. But there was one condition noted on it, two small words that made a world of difference: *Except Iran*.

For as long as those two words were printed on the document, I was forbidden to ever visit my family's home.

When we left Al-Tash camp, we were designated as programme refugees: we had fled Iran because of the war, and because it wasn't safe for us to return, we had been accepted into Ireland's resettlement programme. I'm not sure why the government felt the need to mark our documents so that we couldn't ever travel to Iran. At the time, it wasn't overly important to me. I was a child, and my family had no immediate intention of visiting Kurdistan. But as I got older, one by one my brothers and my parents got the restriction removed so that they could travel to see our relatives, and I knew that I would like to do the same some day. I wrote to the Department of Justice to ask them to remove the endorsement, and when they reissued my travel document, it was gone.

My next stop was the Iranian Embassy. When I arrived for my visa appointment and met the officer assigned to my case, he told me that he already knew me – not just me, but my whole family. He remembered my dad from when he was getting his own paperwork in order. The officer ran through his questions until he was happy, and then he stamped my document: I was officially approved to travel to Iran.

I visited Kurdistan for the first time in June 2015. I regret not going sooner but it never felt like the time was right. There was no point in going for a week; by the time I got there, it would be time to come home again. I needed to go for a month to really make it worthwhile, but there weren't many free months in the calendar: I didn't want to miss work, or too many matches. In the end, I knew that if I didn't go quickly, I would have even more regrets. My grandparents were both in their nineties, and I wanted to spend some time with them while I still could.

I felt that I already knew Zahaw, even though there was no way that I could have. I had heard so many stories over the years, seen so many photographs and watched so many videos. I was excited to finally be there, to see it for myself and breathe in the air and look up into those beautiful mountains. But I didn't really know what to expect, if I'm being honest. I knew that my family loved this place dearly, but at the same time, my picture of Middle Eastern life had been shaped by my time in the West. The impression we're given here is often very one-sided and not the most complimentary: we're told that, outside the super-rich oil regions, it's poor, it's under-developed, and it's dangerous.

I had a conversation one evening with a lad I know up in Thomas Davis. 'Zak, c'mere,' he said, calling me over. 'I was down in your neck of the woods there recently.'

'Where? Leitrim?' I said, trying to beat him to the punchline of his own joke.

He shook his head. 'No, not Leitrim. I was in Tehran.'

'Oh yeah? How did you get on? Was it good craic?'

'That's my third time going over. I love it,' he told me. 'The people are all sound. Listening to the Western media, they have yis all down as bleedin' terrorists.' I'm not surprised that he had a great time. Iran has plenty to offer tourists, as long as they don't mind it being illegal to have a drink. But unfortunately, the stereotypes have stuck.

My brother Raoof travelled over with me that summer. He loves visiting; he tries to go every six months if he can. We flew into Kermanshah Airport, where my uncles were waiting to collect us. On the drive back to Zahaw, we stopped off to get some food. I was suddenly feeling very hungry and I ordered a chicken shish kebab. Raoof was laughing at me.

'Zak, you know it's six o'clock in the morning? This is breakfast.'

We had been travelling for more than a day, with a seven-hour layover in Istanbul, another nine hours between Tehran and Kermanshah, and my body clock was all over the place. It was broad daylight and, as I took a bite of my kebab, I could have sworn it was six in the evening, not six in the morning. I was totally confused.

Nobody ever takes these family visits for granted. Whether we're going to Kurdistan, or one of the uncles or aunties or cousins is coming to Europe, any visit is a huge occasion and a time of great celebration for all the family. My dad had four brothers and two sisters, and all my uncles had big families of their own, so there were a lot of people to catch up with. We got such a warm welcome when we arrived in Zahaw – so warm that we were awake until all hours. I was still up chatting to some of my cousins at three or four in the morning before I finally saw sense and dragged myself off to bed.

Kurdish people don't understand what a lie-in is – at least, my family certainly don't. A lot of the older generation also have a terrible habit of showing up at your house unannounced at any time of the day or night. The next morning, one of my uncles was knocking on our door at eight o'clock.

'Zak, are you awake? Your uncles are on their way,' he called up to me.

'It's eight o'clock. I'm not getting out of bed. I'm shattered after all the travelling. I need a bit of rest.'

'That's very disrespectful.' He was getting a bit annoyed with me. 'You have to get out of bed.'

'I don't care who it is. Tell them to come back later on this afternoon.'

'Oh no, you have to get out of bed,' he said. 'It's very bad manners, very disrespectful. Your uncles are coming, they're all on their way.'

I made absolutely no effort to move, but my uncle wasn't done yet. He went and filled a glass full of cold water and splashed it in my face.

'Come on, get up, you'll be okay. We get up early here. We've been up since six o'clock, we have our day's work nearly done.' In the end, it was easier to give in. I wasn't going to be allowed to go back asleep one way or another.

Being in Zahaw felt familiar, even though I had never been there before. For the first time since leaving Al-Tash camp, I was immersed in Kurdish life, surrounded by Kurdish people. If I wanted to teach a person about the Kurds and our culture, somewhere like this would be the place to do it. Every part of life there, from the clothes my family wear to the food they eat, is so proudly Kurdish. I recognised different smells and tastes. They brought back memories and transported me back to my childhood in the camp. I saw how our life might have been, if only we had been free to live it.

It was in Zahaw that I noticed I had become incredibly Irish in one respect: I could not handle the heat. It was the height of summer, getting up close to forty degrees some days. I hadn't been in heat like that for thirteen years and my body had forgotten what it was like. Indoors, it was fine – all my uncles have air conditioning in their houses, and at that time of year, it's running all the time – but as soon as I stepped out of the front door, I was soaked in sweat. Some days, I needed to have four showers. For my uncles, the heat was normal. I noticed that practically all the men were wearing white shirts, and as the sun beat down on us, I realised why: the light colours are so much cooler in this weather. I looked in my bag; I hadn't packed a single white shirt.

I called up to see my grandparents every day. It was very emotional, meeting them for the first time, seeing their faces and giving them a big hug. There are a lot of different feelings. It's hard not to be a little bit angry at the world that has done this to you, that has forced you apart for more than twenty years. But any tears are happy tears. In the moment, all you feel is love.

My grandparents lived in a house on top of a hill, looking down over the rest of the farm. In the kitchen, the only appliance was a small fridge, and a gas bottle that they used whenever they wanted to cook. They didn't have beds in the house; they wouldn't have any use for them. They preferred to sleep on the ground on a rug as they had always done. My uncles' houses are all big, beautiful, modern places but my grandparents were happy to live in a very simple, traditional way. That was all they wanted from life.

They wanted to hear all about my life in Ireland, what I was doing and how I was getting on, if I liked it there. I had tried to bring a hurl and sliotar out with me so that I could teach them a little about the GAA, but in the end, I had to abandon that plan. I brought my hurl to the airport with me, jammed into the biggest bag that I had, but it was too awkward to be carting around the place. I was dreading the thought of having to keep taking it out at check-in and security, unpacking and re-packing it. The trip was already going to be long enough without adding another headache. It was easier to leave it behind.

I sat down with my grandparents and told them all about this new sport that I had fallen in love with in Ireland.

When I described it to them, they kept telling me about a traditional Kurdish sport that I had never heard of, and asking me if it was the same thing. 'It's similar,' I said, but I hadn't a clue really. It didn't matter if they really understood what I was telling them. They'd never need to know the difference between a sideline cut and a 65. What mattered was that they could see how happy I was, and how much this funny-looking game with the helmets and the sticks meant to me.

I could quickly see why a week's visit back to Kurdistan would never be long enough, and why a month barely was. Every evening, we were invited by one of my uncles to their house. We'd spend the whole evening there, eating dinner together, chatting, playing cards until it got late. The next night, a different uncle would invite us. The night after that, a different uncle again. We never wanted to be rude or disrespectful by missing an invitation; it took us weeks to get around all the different houses.

I wanted to be a tourist as well, and explore Kurdistan for myself. We took a three-hour drive up into the mountains to a city called Sanandaj. We didn't have family there but it was a place I was very keen to visit. The city itself is quite big – about 400,000 people live there – and set into the mountains. As we got closer, I was staring out of the window in disbelief at the areas that we were passing through. The landscape and the scenery were absolutely stunning. When we arrived, we were nearly a kilometre higher than Zahaw.

The heat was nowhere near as exhausting. The mountain air felt fresher. It was a beautiful place.

The one place I couldn't bring myself to visit was my dad's grave. The place in the village where he is buried was pointed out to me, and I had a look from a distance, but I didn't want to go any closer than that. It was enough for me to be there and see it. I don't know if I will ever be able to visit his grave. I'd find it too upsetting. I miss him too much.

SO NEAR
YET SO FAR

T here was a new face at Leitrim training when we went back ahead of the 2015 season. If Martin was at the heart of that core group of people who had given everything to keep Leitrim hurling going, Michael Coleman was the man who wanted to take it to the next level.

Michael needed no introduction as our new trainer: a Galway hurling legend, starting midfielder on that great Galway team of 1988 that made it back-to-back All-Ireland titles for the county, and a three-time All-Star as well for good measure. Martin was still the manager, but to his credit, he didn't have any problem bringing another strong voice into his backroom team if that was what we needed. Sometimes, when the same group have been working together for a while, you can get a new spark of energy from somebody you don't know. An outsider brings fresh ideas, a fresh perspective – and Michael wasn't just any old outsider brought in for the sake of it. He had the CV to back it up. From the moment he arrived in the set-up, he had the respect of the entire panel.

All of Martin's backroom team worked well together, but I could see how Michael and Martin would complement each other nicely. Martin was a real character. He knew us all well. He could sense when we needed an arm around the shoulder rather than a kick up the arse, and he was always ready for a bit of a chat and a bit of craic. Michael was all business: he'd come in, get the session set up, get us working and go. He was there to do a job and he was there to get results; he wanted to improve us.

Some coaches and trainers in the GAA only have eyes for the big jobs. Michael saw the glory in coming to a weaker county, helping a squad to progress and develop, and hopefully, in time, start to challenge for some honours. People looked at him travelling all the way from Galway a couple of times a week, and assumed that somebody must be making it worth his while financially, but he wasn't getting paid to train us. He got the same mileage expenses as anyone else and that was it. He did it all voluntarily, for the love of it.

He had a massive impact. It didn't happen overnight, but session by session, week by week, he transformed us.

When you strip it all back, hurling is a simple game really. Being able to hurl well – the actual touch and skills and mechanics of the game – is the most fundamental thing for any player; when you have that, you can add fitness; when you're fit, you can start to think about tactics. That's exactly how Michael approached things with us. He came in, took one look at us, and saw straight away what we could do to improve. We'd arrive down to training and he'd send us off to do laps around the pitch before we even picked up a hurl. It was very old school, but he didn't care if anyone was looking at him thinking that it was too basic or that it had gone out of fashion in the nineties. He knew what we needed, and he did what he had to do.

I don't think any player likes running sessions at training. I remember slagging one of my friends who plays club football in Dublin after a game in which he'd missed three goal chances, and I'll never forget his response: 'It's not my fault I joined an athletics club.' As many wise men have said, there's no point in being the fittest man on the pitch if you can't strike a ball, and Michael understood that too. We never focused on one thing at the expense of another. We did laps, and we hurled, and we did more laps, and we did more hurling.

We improved tactically too. For as long as I'd been involved, we had been blessed to have two great forwards in Clement Cunniffe and Colm Moreton. Physically, they were two monsters, big, strong, powerful men who would give any defender sleepless nights. They both had a great eye for goal too so, whether it was the first minute or the seventieth, every one of our players knew that if we could get the ball into their hands, there was a chance of them doing damage. Before Michael, one of our favourite tactics was the obvious one: we'd win the ball, we'd drive it long towards them, and we'd bank on them coming off better in more fifty-fifties than not. Our opponents figured us out eventually; once they started to play two defenders in front of Clement or Colm, our route one approach was on borrowed time.

There would always be a time and a place for that traditional direct style, but Michael tried to get it out of our system so that it wasn't our only way of playing. He drilled it into us to be a bit smarter: play off the shoulder; try to find a team-mate in a better position and get the ball into their hand; if we had to go long, play into the corners and try to open up the pitch a bit and create a bit of space. He'd watch every pass while we trained and roar reminders at us from the sideline:

'Give the ball to a man in a better position!'

'Do the simple thing!'

As we got to know Michael and he got to know us, he wasn't afraid to change things around, to move lads into different positions to find the right fit, or to try new tactics. When our opponents got used to us playing 15 on 15, man to man, Michael changed it up and pulled one of the forwards back into defence to play as a sweeper. We didn't score as many goals because we were a man short up front, but we were more solid at the back and we scored more points because our defenders were hoovering up loose balls and winning turnovers and using them to set up scores. When teams started to cop on to that, Michael changed things up again. He never wanted us to be predictable; he always wanted to keep the opposition guessing.

There was one other message that Martin in particular drilled into us: whatever you do, do not get sent off. We were finding it hard enough to win games with fifteen on the pitch; trying to do it with fourteen or thirteen would only add another complication. Martin wasn't warning us because we had a discipline problem; it was coming from years of frustration watching Division 3 hurling and overly fussy referees.

Watch a Division 3 game of hurling, and watch a Division 1 game, and you'll see his point. This isn't a criticism of the standard of refereeing – it's a thankless job, and referees go out to do their best like the rest of us on the pitch – but it's a question of their approach. In the lower tiers, our games are never allowed to flow like they are on a Croke Park Sunday when it's two of the top teams going toe-to-toe. The game we're expected to play is practically a non-contact sport. Everything is a free, every little nudge and shoulder. It's stop-start for seventy minutes, and too many times, the games just became a glorified free-taking contest.

It used to drive Michael mad on the sidelines. This is a man who played on the biggest days against the best in the game, and he would be scratching his head. 'There's not even one free on that pitch. What is he blowing the whistle for?' The yellow cards would slowly add up, and then yellows became reds, and lads – from both sides – ended up getting sent off for absolutely nothing. This wasn't just our problem; it was everybody's. There were times when the corner-back marking me would turn to me in frustration – 'What is your man at today? Would he not just let us play the game?' – and he'd have taken the words right out of my mouth.

It's not entirely the referees' fault either. At one of our games, I spotted a referee I knew from Dublin and went over to chat to him. I knew who was down to ref our game, and it wasn't him.

'What are you down here for?' I asked him.

'I'm here to do an assessment,' he told me, and I knew straight away that we would be in for a long day. We dreaded seeing the referees' assessor sitting up in the stands with their pen and paper. They scrutinised every decision to make a note of it all in their report, and if a referee ever had any ambition to progress to a higher level than Division 3, they needed to get a glowing review. Every little rule would be refereed to the letter of the law with no room for common sense. Someone might argue that that's exactly how it should be, and what's the point in having rules if you're not going to enforce them, and that's fair enough. But let me tell you one thing, it doesn't make for an entertaining game of hurling when the play is stopped every thirty seconds over nothing.

Sometimes you'd have a referee who was just starting to get matches at Division 1 level, but still refereeing some of our games as well. I'd watch them refereeing a big league or championship match in Nowlan Park or Semple Stadium, and it was like watching a completely different referee.

'When it's one of the big counties playing, you never blow your whistle,' I said to him during a match one day. 'You're blowing it every minute here.'

'I'm being watched,' he said, and that was it.

More important than any of the changes that Martin and Michael made to our training and our tactics was the way they brought us together as a team. Apart from a couple of blow-ins like me, the panel was almost entirely made up of lads from either Carrick or Manorhamilton – that comes with the territory when you're a small county with only a handful of senior clubs – but the rivalry between these two clubs is as fierce as you'll find anywhere. In the early days, I could see it carrying over into the county set-up and it was holding us back a bit: the two clubs would meet in a big local derby, either a league final or a county final, and they'd knock lumps out of each other, and the bruises would still be fresh when we all linked up with Leitrim the following week. The Carrick lads would stick with the Carrick lads, and the Manor lads would stick with the Manor lads, and I'd be in the middle slagging them. 'Come on, lads, would you ever mix in a little bit?'

Martin and Michael got the message through to us: we train as one group, we play as one group, and when you're with Leitrim, you leave your club allegiances in the car park. The Carrick and Manor lads would still get properly stuck in when they met in a club match, and I'd bring the popcorn, but with Leitrim, we were a team.

On the pitch, it felt like we had built on the positives of our 2014 league campaign and taken another step forward in 2015 with Michael's help. The results proved that; in the end, we were only two pucks of two balls away from playing in two finals. The margins were as fine as ever. After starting with a defeat to Longford and a win over Sligo, we went into our last league game knowing that a win away in Warwickshire would be good enough to see us back into the Division 3B final for a second straight year. The game was still up for grabs inside the final few minutes until they got two late scores to edge us out by a single point, 3-18 to 4-14.

That season's Lory Meagher campaign was even more heart-breaking because the prize on offer was something bigger than a trip to Ashbourne for a league final. Not long after we first arrived in Carrick-on-Shannon, a reporter from the *Irish Daily Mail* came down to the club to speak with me for an interview. I was still learning English so Mokhtar came along as well to translate for me. I was thirteen, and I'd been living in Ireland a little over a year, but when the reporter asked me if I had any ambitions, I was already sure of my answer: I wanted to play for Leitrim in Croke Park some day.

We all did, every single player on that panel, and the prospect was dangled in front of us as we headed to play Fermanagh in our last match of the round-robin series. We had already beaten both of the Exiles, Warwickshire and Lancashire, and a third win would be enough to send us to Croke Park. I got a goal early in the second half to push us into a five-point lead but before we even dared to start dreaming, Fermanagh had pegged us back. Only for a missed penalty, they would have pulled clear of us even sooner. They were three points up heading into the final moments and, for the second time that season, we found ourselves in a one-score game with a place in the final on the line and time slipping through our fingers.

We threw everything at them in the hope of carving open some space to give us one last good sight on goal and the chance of an equaliser, but it never came. A draw might well have been good enough for us when the final league table was all added up but Fermanagh were three-point winners, 2-14 to 1-14. They could start making their plans for Croke Park; but for all of us in Leitrim, the dream would have to wait a little longer.

THE PROMISED LAND

I logged on to the GAA website when I heard that the Lory Meagher All-Star team for 2016 had been announced. As a group we hadn't had the best championship, winning just one of our four games, but I was curious to see who had been picked as the best fifteen of the year, and if any of the lads had caught the selectors' eye.

I was halfway down the list when I spotted Colm Moreton's name, which was well-deserved recognition, but I had to do a double-take when I saw the next name after his: I had won an All-Star too.

I was astonished. I hadn't even considered that I might be in the running. At the same time, I felt I was hurling really well that season and that my game was in a really good place. I was twenty-five, which is when a lot of hurlers are said to be coming into their best years, and maybe that was true for me. I was hurling well with Thomas Davis too, and I won Player of the Year there as well in the club's end-of-season awards.

I scored from play in all four of our Lory Meagher games that season, even the ones where I only got a run off the bench as a sub. That can't have hurt my cause, but other than that, I didn't feel I was doing anything particularly new with my game that would make me stand out from the crowd. The main difference was that I was really able to commit to my hurling. I was still doing a few shifts in the bar up in the club, and working for Kingsbury Furniture in Tallaght as well, helping with deliveries. I was lucky to have a lot of flexibility in both jobs; it gave me the opportunity to train as much as I wanted to, and I never had to worry about missing a match, and that consistency definitely shone through in my performances on the pitch.

Colm and I got the tuxedos on a few days later and made our way to the All-Star awards night in the Convention Centre in Dublin. It was a huge honour to be there, both for ourselves individually and as representatives of our team-mates and of Leitrim hurling in general. I had never been at the All-Stars before and I had a brilliant night, meeting players from other counties and having a drink and a bit of a chat. At that time, most people in the GAA didn't know who I was, but it was easy to see that I stood out from all of the other players who had won awards that night. People in

Leitrim knew my story and people in the club did too, but up until then, not many others knew that there was a Kurdish-Irish refugee hurling for Leitrim.

I loved telling people about my life – it doesn't leave you short of something to chat about anyway. Over the years, I had just hurled away and there was never much fuss or attention about my background. Because I have quite a strong Irish accent, most people presumed that I had been born in Ireland and lived my whole life here. A few people thought that I might have been adopted as a child. When I told stories about what it was like for me growing up and where I had come from and how I had got here, people were genuinely interested and curious, which was really nice. The GAA is their life, and it didn't take long for them to see that it is every bit as important to me, that it had become my life too.

When the new season started with Leitrim in 2017, we had every reason to think that we could take the next few steps in our development, not only to do something that had never been done before by taking a Leitrim hurling team to an All-Ireland final in Croke Park, but to go one better than that: to win it. There were only six teams in the Lory Meagher and there was very little to choose between us all. In any given season, one of the six might stand out as the favourites, another might struggle, but there would only really be a point or two to separate the rest of us. We weren't looking over our shoulder any more, desperate for one win to keep us off the bottom of the table. We were building something. We had improved so much in the two previous seasons, and now this was our time. The championship was there to be won, but we had to believe that we were good enough to do it.

We were on the right path, but our first game, away to Fermanagh, showed us that we still had a way to go, and that nothing would be easily won. We were six points up with ten minutes to play, and we ended up losing by a point. We were shellshocked at full time, but we didn't let it derail us. We got back on track with good wins against Cavan and Lancashire, and despite losing in Warwickshire, we were still alive going into the final round of matches. The situation was the same as it had been for us so many times in the past, one make-or-break match. It wasn't quite as simple as win and we're in – we'd still need to keep an eye on the results elsewhere – but we knew that none of the other games would matter unless we did our own job first. If we wanted to go to Croke Park, we had to beat Sligo.

We started at a million miles an hour, as if we were trying to kill the game stone dead before it even got started. We very nearly managed it. We totally blitzed Sligo, scoring 2-3 in the first six minutes, while they barely managed to get a shot away, never mind their first score. There was no way that we could sustain that pace or that intensity for seventy minutes, and as our performance dropped a level or two, Sligo stepped up their own. By half time, our early lead was as good as gone; they were only a point behind us.

We had been here before – not just against Fermanagh, but so many times in previous seasons too. We left the door open for teams, let leads slip away, lost games that we were definitely good enough to have won, and lived to regret it. Not today. Not when the stakes were so high. We pushed on again at the start of the second half but Sligo's season was on the line too, and they wouldn't give in without a fight. We were still only three points up coming into the final few minutes and nowhere near comfortable until the ball broke to me late on. I saw my chance and took it. I squeezed the ball over the line for the goal that made the game safe. The referee blew his whistle a couple of moments later. We could breathe again. We could finally start to believe it. The Leitrim hurlers were going to Croke Park.

This day had been a long time coming and we made sure to enjoy it. 'The promised land,' Martin said in his interviews afterwards, and he was speaking for every one of us. This really was the promised land. Getting to the Lory Meagher final was about more than just a single game. It was more than just us proving to ourselves that we were good enough, that we wouldn't always crumble under the pressure when the tough questions were asked, that we had the right to believe in a better future for Leitrim hurling. It was a culmination of everything we'd worked for since I first joined the panel in 2012, when we were losing games by thirty-three points and Martin was telling us that it wouldn't always be like this, that we could get better, one point at a time. This journey had started long before me. Lads like Clement Cunniffe, James Glancy and Vinny McDermott had carried the candle for Leitrim hurling when it was only a flicker in the dark. Everything we had worked for, every drive to training, every night out that we had said no to, had led us to this moment. Now that we were here, we had no intention of stopping.

There was a three-week break between the final round-robin matches and the championship final, and for that entire time, there was the most amazing buzz around the squad. For so many years, Leitrim had been hurling in the shadows where nobody could see us. We were excited if we even saw as much as a ten-second clip of a Division 3 or Lory Meagher match on *The Sunday Game* – it didn't even particularly matter if it was one of our games or not. Now we felt as though we were in the spotlight. Journalists and photographers were at our training sessions. There were interviews and features in the papers and on the internet. We agreed to practically every media request that came in; we didn't want to miss an opportunity to put the county on the map, to let everyone see that yes, there was hurling in Leitrim, and we were fiercely proud of it.

We knew that Warwickshire were the favourites for the final. Everything about this adventure was new to us but they had been there, done that, and probably still had the

2013 Lory Meagher Champions T-shirts put away in a drawer somewhere at home. Our lads had never even played in Croke Park, never mind climbed the steps of the Hogan Stand to lift a cup. Warwickshire already held plenty of advantages over us, and they had one more ace in their hand: Liam Watson. Watson had been one of the best hurlers in Antrim before he moved to England, and now he was their star man. He was a lethal free-taker on top of everything else. When we played Warwickshire in the round-robin series, not even a month before the final, we got a lesson in how he could punish us. He scored seven points, and Warwickshire beat us that day by eight.

Watson was the difference again in the final, but he wasn't the only difference. We were well beaten in the end. It was an incredible feeling to come out of the tunnel and run out onto the Croke Park pitch, hearing the roar of all the Leitrim fans who had travelled up to support us, looking up and seeing their part of the stand blanketed in green and gold. But Martin had been hammering one point into us since the semi-final over and over again: Croke Park isn't the place for just showing up so that you can tell your grandkids some day that you played there. Croke Park is for winning. Finals are for winning. And we didn't do that. After all the build-up and buzz and excitement, we just didn't perform on the day. It's the most disappointing feeling of all to walk away from the biggest game of your career and know that you could have done better. It's crushing.

For thirty-five minutes, we matched Warwickshire, but the game lasts a lot longer than that, and half a performance is no use to anybody. We were two points up at half time, but we fell apart in the second half. We were totally flat and couldn't get into the tempo of the game at all. We only managed one point, and down the other end Watson was killing us with his free-taking, as we knew he would if he was given a chance. Between ourselves and the referee, we gave him plenty of chances; Watson finished with 0-11 from frees, nearly two-thirds of Warwickshire's total points. Any hope we had of a late rally to turn things around was wiped out by two red cards in the space of a couple of minutes, first for Colm, and then for Dave McGovern. They were two very soft reds for the referee to give. We lost by six points in the end, 0-17 to 0-11, and there was plenty of blame to lay at our own performance before we started trying to point the finger at anyone else.

When you lose like that, you analyse everything. You look at the game, your performance, your preparation, every possible angle, over and over again, to try to find the things you could have done differently. We weren't fit enough, for one thing. Michael had done everything he could to prepare us for the sheer size of the Croke Park pitch, but there was too much ground for us to cover, and we struggled. Warwickshire were fitter, they were more experienced, they had a dynamite free-taker and, in the end, they were a better team than us that day.

We didn't handle the occasion well either. We weren't used to being in finals. We were used to our usual pre-match routine, but that had all changed. We had met in Dublin the day before and stayed in the Maldron Hotel that night, but I don't think one of us got a proper night's sleep. The nerves and the adrenaline had all mixed into one at that point. Three, maybe four hours, that seemed to be the case for everyone. It didn't do us any favours. You try to console yourself with the thought that there will be another chance, that you'll be back again next year for another shot at it and that you can do things differently then, that you won't make the same mistakes again. You have to think that way – there's not much point in playing if you don't believe that – but the reality is that there might not be another chance. There's no guarantee.

While Warwickshire lifted the cup and made their speech and got their party started, our bus was waiting for us underneath the stand. We went in to Ryan's on Camden Street to have a couple of pints. Ryan's have been great supporters of Leitrim hurling over the years, and the place was absolutely packed out with Leitrim fans when we went in. Although we were devastated that we hadn't given them the day that they deserved, they made sure we knew how proud they were. We were representing them and the county as a whole when we pulled on that jersey, and we had done something that no other Leitrim hurling side had ever done.

Most importantly, we had shown a whole generation of young kids that it was possible to hurl for Leitrim and to play in Croke Park some day. That was our dream. Now it could be their dream too.

AT LAST

I missed the 2017 Dublin intermediate championship final with Thomas Davis. It's one of the few regrets I have, even though I couldn't have done anything differently.

People sometimes underestimate how hard it can be to win a league or championship at intermediate level. It is exceptionally tough. Every single game is a dog fight because every single team is trying to get out of there and get promoted up to senior. When the championship came around that year, we were flying. We got off to the best possible start and topped our group with three wins from three, but we felt we would only really know where we stood after our next game: away to Kevin's.

Every time we played each other, it wasn't just a battle. There was an edge to it too. The two clubs are about twenty minutes apart, so it's not exactly a local derby, but there was a fierce rivalry between us, particularly after what had happened in the 2010 final. At the start of a season, we'd have it in the back of our heads that if we were going to win anything, we would have to go through Kevin's at some stage to get there – and that if we did beat them, it wasn't much good squeezing past them by a point. We wanted to beat them back out the gate. If we could do that, then we had every right to believe that we were on the right track.

For around forty-five minutes against them that day, I didn't touch the ball. That's not an exaggeration; I don't remember having a single touch. It was a rough game, and a messy game, and the lad who was marking me thought he was having a stormer. He got out in front of me a good few times to win the ball, and he must have thought that he had me in his pocket for the rest of the evening.

Shane Plowman, our old manager, had once told me that if I couldn't get into a game, the most important thing was to just keep moving. It's a defender's dream if you stand there. You couldn't be making their life any easier. Anyone can mark a statue. Shane's words stuck with me, and that's what I did – I kept moving. For as long as I was left on the pitch, I just kept going. At the same time, my marker started getting a bit excited and carried away with himself. He started to go forward a bit more, leaving me alone and sometimes nearly forgetting about me altogether.

I scored 3-3 in the last fifteen minutes to win us the game. I always think of it as one of my best ever performances for the club – it's certainly one that sticks out in my memory – but the rest of the lads let me know exactly what they thought afterwards.

'That's the worst performance we've ever seen. You were absolutely useless for forty-five minutes.'

They had a point, even if they were only winding me up, but those forty-five minutes didn't matter in the end. Shane was right. I only needed to be lucky once. I just got very lucky that evening.

We won our last game against Ballyboden to make sure we topped the group with an unbeaten record, and when the knockout rounds started in September, we beat St Vincent's in the quarter-finals. A few days before the semis against St Peregrine's, a shooting pain suddenly started to rip through my stomach. I've never felt anything like it, either before or since. I was in agony and before I knew it, I was in Tallaght Hospital, begging for somebody to do something to help me.

'It's only pain,' the doctor told me initially. 'You probably ate something. Just take these and you'll be fine.' But I needed something stronger than a couple of Panadol or whatever it was they were giving me. I was in bits, doubled over, unable to even stand up straight. I tried to explain that this wasn't a dodgy stomach, that there was something seriously wrong with me, but the doctors and nurses were run off their feet and I was way down their list of priorities. It felt like an eternity before they even found a bed for me so that I could lie down, and when I did, another doctor came to assess me and started pressing on different parts of my stomach.

'Is it sore there?'

We didn't need to go through this. 'Everywhere. It's sore everywhere,' I said. 'There's definitely something wrong with me.' Eventually, it became clear that there was a problem with my appendix and that it needed to come out.

'You'll have to wait until tomorrow,' the doctor told me. 'We won't be able to do the surgery until then.'

I would have taken it out there and then myself if I could have. The only thing that was even slightly distracting me from the pain was the thought of our semi-final on Saturday. All I wanted to do was to play against Peregrine's, but once I was told that I needed surgery, I had to admit defeat. I texted Johnny McGlynn, our manager, to let him know that I wouldn't be able to make it.

The operation went well and by Saturday afternoon I was doing everything I could to convince the doctors and nurses to send me home. Our match was down for a five o'clock throw-in and if I got discharged quickly enough, I'd still be in enough time to make it.

'You need to take it easy for a couple of days,' they warned me when they agreed to let me go. 'Just sit at home for a couple of days. Don't go anywhere.'

When I walked out of the front door of the hospital, the first thing I did was jump into a taxi and ask the driver to take me straight up to the club. There wasn't a hope in hell that I could have played; I was in bits just standing on the sideline and shouting for the lads, but it was worth it; we pulled off a comeback in the second half and beat Peregrine's by two points.

Now I was in a race against the clock. The final, against Na Fianna in Parnell Park, was a fortnight away, and I was desperate to be fit in time to play. I tried to get myself right but I was only kidding myself. Two weeks was nowhere near enough time, no matter how badly I wanted it. I had absolutely no energy at all, but I convinced Johnny that I was okay to tog out for the final and to include me as a sub.

'If you need me, and you want to bring me on, I'm there,' I told him, but one look at my face told Johnny everything he needed to know about how much I would really be able to offer on the pitch. He never even considered bringing me on, and it was without a doubt the right decision. We couldn't afford any passengers if we wanted to beat Na Fianna. The final was a low-scoring game with very little between us, but as it crept towards a draw, Kevin Ward popped up with a late, late point to win us the championship.

We had been waiting seven years to get back to this point, seven years to right the wrongs of 2010 and put those bad memories to bed, and now we could finally enjoy it the way we were supposed to: no controversy, no appeals, no half-hearted celebrations in the clubhouse a few days later; just pure happiness out there on the Parnell Park pitch with the cup in our hands.

Nights like that don't come around too often. We had earned every last bit of it. I just wish I could have fully enjoyed the celebrations. The pints flowed all night and into the next day and beyond, but I couldn't even face a drink. I had tried my best to get fit, but in the end, I was only fit enough for one thing, and that was to be at home in my bed.

REBUILDING

It was a Sunday night in November when the earthquake destroyed Zahaw. The tremors were felt across the Middle East. It measured 7.3 on the Richter Scale, one of the most powerful earthquakes anywhere in the world in 2017. As people dug through the rubble in search of their loved ones and pulled bodies out from the wreckage of collapsed buildings, it became clear that it had also been the deadliest.

My brother Mokhtar was on the phone to one of my uncles when the ground started shaking. Tremors and earthquakes are common in Iran and, at first, we didn't know how serious this one would turn out to be. We were thousands of miles away, and the initial information was the most basic: there had been a massive earthquake across Iran and Iraq. Kermanshah province, and Zahaw, had been among the worst affected. As the scale of the tragedy started to become clear, the first reports suggested that at least five hundred people had been killed and more than 7,000 others had been injured. The true numbers might never be fully known.

Zahaw was flattened. It was nighttime when the earthquake hit, and people couldn't react as quickly as they might have during the day. We didn't know who was safe, who needed help. We lost family in the disaster. My dad's first cousin was asleep when the earthquake hit. He couldn't get out of his house in time and died. Many more of our relatives suffered injuries. One of my uncles was crushed and had to be flown by helicopter to hospital in Tehran for treatment. Even for those who escaped without any serious injuries, their houses were destroyed. It was too dangerous to even be near the ruins of the buildings; the aftershocks kept coming in the days after the first earthquake. It was winter and the temperatures were dropping close to freezing once the sun went down. They had nowhere safe to sleep indoors so they slept outside, or in tents, in the cold.

Every new picture and video that we saw showed more devastation. Landslides were blocking some roads and making it difficult for emergency teams to get through to the areas where they were badly needed. The hospitals were overwhelmed. This was a humanitarian crisis. They needed help now.

So many Kurdish-Irish families had relatives caught up in the tragedy. We did whatever we could, but we felt so helpless from far away. I did an interview to raise awareness among people here in Ireland, to try to explain just how catastrophic the situation was. We contacted the Iranian ambassador in Dublin and urged him to request government help as quickly as possible.

Ayatollah Ali Khamenei visited Kermanshah in the days after the earthquake and pleaded with the people of Iran to help where they could. Helicopters delivered tents and blankets and food and water, the basics for survival. Volunteers packed up their cars with essentials and drove towards the suffering; people gave money to charities and the aid organisations. Ali Daei, the legendary Iranian footballer, and Sadegh Zibakalam, one of the country's top academics, gathered donations from people across the country to send to the areas that needed it most. And when the time came to start the hard work of rebuilding the cities and towns and villages in Kermanshah and beyond, help was there for that too. The Iranian government got to work repairing the cracked and shattered roads. The city of Zahaw was rebuilt too for the second time in the space of forty years, for the second time in my relatives' lives there. They moved into their new houses on the farm, and my uncles finally persuaded my grandmother to leave her house on the top of the hill and come down to live with them.

Help came from all over Iran; from Farsi people, Arab people, thousands of them, tens of thousands. For so many years, Iran had been divided by cultural, political and religious differences, but in the aftermath of the earthquake, when they needed to come together, so many were united behind a common cause. In times of great tragedy, people will always be there for each other.

MONEY TALKS

Our breakthrough with Leitrim didn't come in 2018. That year it was the same old story, another late lead thrown away, another year of heartbreak in the league final.

Up until then, it had been another solid year for us in Division 3B. We won three of our four games, and with the one that we lost – a one-point defeat against Lancashire – we had a chance to make up for it quickly when we played them again for the league title. The final was one that got away from us, although it didn't help that we were missing two of our best players. James was ruled out through injury, and as the final got closer, it became clear that we wouldn't have Colm either. He had decided to play both football and hurling that year, and so had only played in one of our round-robin games. There was another fixture clash on the day of the final: the footballers were playing Wicklow that same afternoon. They were already out of the running for a place in their own league final, and we had a shot at a national title. We needed our best possible starting fifteen available, and Colm was a game-changing player for us, but despite Martin's best efforts and a few tense words with the football management, we had to do it without him in the end.

In such a tight final, it doesn't take much imagination to wonder what difference James and Colm might have made to us. We played most of the game with fourteen men after Kevin McGrath was sent off in the first half. Having been three points down at half time, we put in a huge performance in the second half to claw our way back and lead by three with just three minutes to play. We had given everything to get ourselves into that position and we had nothing more left to give. We were out on our feet. Lancashire got three late points to force extra time. They ran away with the game and we couldn't run after them. It finished 1-25 to 1-18.

That summer's championship brought a new challenge too. Traditionally only the Lory Meagher winners get promoted to the Nicky Rackard Cup, which is the next tier up, but the GAA decided to reshape things in 2018 and send two teams up. As the second-best team the previous season, we got bumped up along with Warwickshire. It was good to test ourselves at that level – it had always been one of our goals to move up to the Nicky Rackard – but we wanted to earn it by winning the Lory Meagher, not by default because of a format change.

We only played three championship games that year and lost all of them, including a relegation play-off against Louth, so we went straight back down again. It was easy to see that the step up had come a little too soon for us. We were still building our team, trying to bring through a few younger players so that we would have more strength in depth. That's exactly what we did. When Martin brought us all together ahead of the new season in 2019, we had our biggest-ever panel with thirty-six or thirty-seven lads at training. We had never seen those kinds of numbers before. It was a huge boost – a squad of that size would put us in a great position to get back to Croke Park and go one step further this time – but we quickly realised that there was no point in getting too excited. Within a few weeks, the county board was already talking about cutting the panel.

We couldn't allow that to happen. We were a team, and nobody on that panel was going to see somebody else thrown under the bus. The county board's motives had nothing to do with hurling. It was purely a financial decision. An extra seven players on the panel meant another seven tracksuits, seven gear bags, seven more mileage claims, seven extra mouths to feed. All of that money adds up and it has to come from somewhere.

'There is no way we are cutting this panel,' Michael

assured all of us. 'If we have to put in money for tracksuits for the rest of the lads, we'll do it ourselves.'

It wouldn't even be a consideration for so many counties. For them, the money is never-ending. They could have a panel of sixty and run off full-squad A versus B matches every week if they wanted, and nobody would bat an eyelid or even notice it in the accounts, but it mattered to us. I understood that the board had their budget and it was their job to make sure that they stuck to it. I didn't blame them for doing their job, but our job was to win a Lory Meagher Cup for Leitrim, and I hoped that they wouldn't blame us for doing ours by pushing back against them.

I went and spoke to Martin McCartin, the treasurer of the Leitrim County Board. I get on great with Martin, and we've worked together a lot over the years, but he's not afraid to stand his ground if he doesn't agree with you.

'The GAA rules say there's thirty players on a panel,' he told me, 'and we're only going by the GAA rules.'

I understood that he was doing an impossible job too. If he's the treasurer, he's like any other accountant: he needs to see money coming in, not going out. He had a lot more than just the Leitrim hurlers to worry about, and very little money to go around. In the end, the county board and management worked out an agreement. The players could stay. We kept our full panel.

I've never had a problem speaking up on behalf of my team-mates. A lot of players don't want the hassle, they just want to concentrate on training and playing and going home to their family, but someone has to do it. You don't need to fall out with people; you just need to fight your corner.

I had already been acting as one of the player reps for our squad for a good few years at that stage. It was James who first got me involved with the Gaelic Players Association. He and Dave McGovern were our two reps, but James had been doing the job for a long time, and he was particularly keen to bring in somebody new to share the workload.

'Will you come to a few of these meetings with me and help me out?' he asked. I didn't really know what was involved.

'Don't worry,' he said. 'You'll like this.'

I went with him to my first meeting in Cathal Brugha Barracks in Rathmines. The meeting started to discuss the players' charter, a list of all of the things that the GPA and the GAA had negotiated and agreed that all inter-county players should be entitled to, whether it was mileage expenses or a boot allowance or other gear. I was taking in everything that was being said.

'We're not really getting anything, are we?' I said to James.

'I know,' he said. 'I told you that you would like this.'

He was our main rep but once I had got my head around everything that was going on, I was happy to ring

Martin McCartin myself to have a chat with him and try to work out some sort of agreement around what support we were getting.

'Tell them that we need to be treated the same as the footballers,' Dave told me. 'If they're getting a tracksuit and they're getting a bag, we just want the same as them. We need the county board to get us some gear. We can't be waiting three or four months for it.'

I rang Martin to discuss it with him. 'The GPA have told us that we're entitled to this, that it has all been agreed,' I explained. 'They told us that the GAA are paying for it.'

Then I tried a different approach. 'The footballers get treated very well. The lads can see that, they have mates on the football team. All they want is to be treated the same. They're not asking for much.'

'There's thirty-six of you,' he reminded me. That was the crux of it as far as he was concerned, but I had made our case to him. At the GPA meetings, I never heard any of the lads from big counties worrying about whether or not their expenses would get paid. The money was always there. The game is a lot easier when you don't have to worry about that, when you just need to turn up and concentrate on doing your job.

I could see Martin's position, though, and in the years that followed, I took it on myself to try to help. We had the Bush Hotel in Carrick as our jersey sponsors at the time, but they were mainly there to sponsor the footballers.

'We don't really have our own sponsor for the hurlers, do we?' I asked Martin one day.

'No, but if you know anybody ...' he said. I didn't have anybody in particular in mind at that point, but I've never been afraid to ask. What's the worst that somebody could say?

I was having a pint in Thomas Davis one night when I got chatting to Derek Tyrrell. Derek owns his own air conditioning company, Tyrrellair. I was explaining the whole situation to him and how we were looking for someone who could give us a bit of help.

'Would you be up for it?' I asked him.

'Of course, yeah, no problem. I'd love to sponsor you.' Tyrrellair's logo was front and centre on the hurling jersey from that point on, and we were very grateful to be wearing it.

When we were hoping to get new track tops for the championship in 2019, I asked Peter Farrell from Ryan's pub on Camden Street if there was anything he could do to help us out. I didn't need to ask him twice.

'How much do you need for them?' he asked me. 'Call back in to me tomorrow and I'll have it here ready for you.'

We tried every possible avenue over the years to bring in whatever money we could. Pauric McWeeney – Smiley, as we call him – had been around the panel for a good long time as well, and one day the two of us were chatting about fundraising.

'Is there anything we could try to organise?' I asked him. 'What do you think?'

Smiley did a huge amount of work and pulled together some brilliant prizes for a big raffle. It was a huge success, all thanks to his efforts, and the money that we raised went a long way in helping to cover the bills. I've seen it with the club as well so many times over the years; someone with a business that's going well is more than happy to help out by chipping in a few quid to buy a few bags of sliotars or whatever is needed. A lot of the time, there's only one condition: just don't go mentioning their name and making a show of them.

It takes a lot of time and energy when you're constantly trying to find enough money here and there to keep a team on the road. We're lucky that there are a lot of decent people out there who love Leitrim hurling as much as we do. We couldn't do it without them.

THE ROAD
TO CROKER

Whenever I was named on the bench, Michael always sent me away with the same instruction.

'Be ready to go on. I'm not going to tell you to go out and warm up, you warm up whenever you need to warm up. But just be ready to go on.'

I was sitting in the Hogan Stand, only taking my eyes off the game to check the big screen that showed the clock and the scoreboard. Neither was in our favour. Lancashire were keeping us at arm's length, and time was quickly running out in the 2019 Lory Meagher final.

I was waiting for Michael's call. I was ready to go on.

*

From the very start of the 2019 season, the competition within the squad had been fierce. It was what we had been crying out for all along: a big panel where every single person was fighting for their place in the starting fifteen. Each training session was an opportunity, an audition. The intensity and the effort that each of us brought as individuals drove us on as a group. Not that you would have known it from our league results that spring: we started out hoping to make it to back-to-back league finals, but we lost all four of our games and finished at the bottom of Division 3B. It was disappointing but we had to draw a line under it quickly. The championship was just around the corner again.

Our forward lines were stacked with options. Clement and Colm were still as dangerous as ever. We had a rock-solid free-taker in Gavin O'Hagan. The two lads from Cork, Cathal O'Donovan and Ben Murray, had brought a whole new threat to our attack since they had joined us in 2017 and 2018. We had Stephen Goldrick, we had Adam Byrne – and we had me. That made at least eight of us fighting it out for the same six starting spots. The numbers didn't add up.

We didn't have a first-choice starting fifteen. Most of the time, we didn't know the line-up until the morning of the game when Martin and Michael would call us all together to give us the team. There were always changes. Nobody was guaranteed to start. That had been Michael's approach from the moment he started working with us. If you weren't performing, you were dropped. He wanted the best players in the best form in every single game. It didn't matter what you had done in the past; it was all about what you could do the next day. I liked that.

Michael could see how the game was changing as well, and he wasn't going to be left behind. It was no longer enough to have a good starting line-up and one or two handy lads on the bench. Hurling had become a squad game, twenty-six versus twenty-six instead of fifteen against fifteen. In all the best teams, at every level, the substitutes were every bit as important as the starters. When a game was getting stretched in the second half and it was there to be won or lost, you needed good lads who could come in and shift the balance back in your favour, lads who would either spark a comeback or close out a win. A manager's priority used to be to make sure their best fifteen was on the pitch at the start of the game; more and more, they were starting to think about the fifteen they would have on at the end as well.

It became clear that was the job that management had in mind for me in 2019; I would be one of the impact subs coming in off the bench. I wanted to do whatever was going to put the team in the best position to win, of course, but I was annoyed that I wasn't starting – I'm a hurler, and I wanted to hurl. For all of my career, I had been a starter rather than a substitute, and you get used to playing all the time. I had never been the lad left standing on the line week after week. I felt like I had a lot more to offer than ten or fifteen minutes at the end of a game.

As I got older myself, I realised the importance of having some experienced and older heads in a squad. So many times, they're the ones you want to be sending into battle when the game is on the line. You can trust that they'll do the right things and make the right decisions and won't panic. But I was still only twenty-eight. I was still full of running. I could see it from Martin and Michael's perspective. I knew what they were trying to do and I respected their decisions, but I found it very frustrating. I picked up a couple of little injuries as well that season, and once that started, I found it very difficult to force my way back into the picture.

Our team WhatsApp group was called 'The Road to Croker'. That had been our mission for so many years, but when we had followed that road all the way to the end in 2017, it hadn't led us to where we wanted to go. Between league and championship, we had lost three finals in the previous five seasons, each one with its own frustrating circumstances and its own regrets and what-might-have-beens. We were knocking on the door, but we were tired of being nearly men. We hadn't won anything yet and we wouldn't be happy until we did.

We tried to run the disappointment of the league campaign out of our system by playing challenge matches nearly every week in the run-up to the championship. We were playing against decent club teams and beating practically all of them, which gave us great confidence as we got on the plane to head for our opening championship match away to Lancashire.

It was a disgrace of a game. We were beaten by two points, 0-20 to 1-15, but from the moment we arrived at the ground in Manchester, everything went against us. It was only afterwards that we realised that the GAA had only appointed one official for the game, the referee, who was from Dublin. For whatever reason, they hadn't bothered to send any linesmen or umpires with him. The referee did his best to keep a handle on things but it was chaos.

If Martin and Michael and the rest of the management team were aware of that beforehand, they didn't say anything to us. We played the game without realising that the ref was the only neutral official there – I certainly did anyway, whatever about anybody else. We were raging on the sideline as the game went on, but when we found out the full story afterwards, there was murder. I've rarely seen a dressing room so angry. This was our championship, and it could have been ruined on the first day because the GAA didn't have enough respect for us, and for Lancashire, to send a full team of officials to our match. We were disgusted by how we had been treated.

There was talk in the papers of a protest and an appeal, but we had to move on from it. We felt that we had been totally let down, but it was one game, and we knew that if we could win our final two matches, that could still be enough to see us through to the final and back to Croke Park. We beat Cavan the following weekend, which set us up for a showdown at home to Fermanagh in our last match. We went into that game knowing exactly what we needed to do: if we beat them by four points, it might be enough; if we beat them by five, it definitely would be; anything less and our season was over again. Five was the number in everyone's head that week. We didn't want there to be any doubt.

A few minutes into the second half, we had our five-point advantage. It's never that simple, though. Fermanagh came back at us and with ten minutes to play, our lead had been cut to a single point. We were back at the bottom of the mountain, and if we were going to climb it, we needed to do it quickly.

We scored one.

And they scored one.

Then we scored one.

And another one.

And another one.

Everybody was frantically checking the score: 2-16 to 1-15. We were four up. We knew the final table would be decided by points scored if we couldn't be separated on points difference. We quickly did the sums to work out what we needed. If the whistle went now, that would be enough, but there was still time left. Besides, we had agreed that our target was five. We wanted one more. One more.

There was a roar from our sideline when Gavin fired over another point, but we couldn't relax. Fermanagh pulled one back to make it a four-point game again, and now they only needed one more point to knock us out and go through themselves. Next point winner was a rule that kids agreed when they were being called home for their dinner, not when there was a place in the Lory Meagher Cup final on the line, but that was the situation that we found ourselves in.

Those final few moments felt like they would last for ever, the time getting slower and slower until it stood still completely, and then Gavin scored one final point. That made five. We were going to Croke Park again – and this time, we were going to win.

DO IT TODAY

We learned a lot about ourselves when we lost the Lory Meagher final in 2017. We promised ourselves that we wouldn't make the same mistakes again.

The weeks leading up to the 2019 final against Lancashire were a lot more low-key. The buzz and excitement was every bit as special, and we savoured every second of it, but the inexperienced Leitrim of two years earlier was nowhere to be seen. We had been through it all before. We knew what to expect now. We knew the rhythm of the day, the layout of the dressing room, the timings for the warm-ups. The mood in the squad was a lot more controlled, a lot more focused. We had a job to do. The main messages in our team meeting the night before the game were all very simple: eat right, drink loads of water, get a good night's sleep. At that stage, there was very little else left to say. It had all been said already.

You never know what it takes to win a championship until you finally get over the line. Martin and Michael, and the rest of the management team, had been constantly reinforcing one thing with us for weeks, the same thing that they had been telling us for years: we were good enough, but we had to believe that ourselves. Really believe. They reminded us of everything that we had already given up to get here, the hours that we had put in, all the sacrifices we had made. It had taken everything we had just to get this far; now we had to dig deep and find something inside ourselves that we didn't even know we had, and give ourselves that one last push to get to the top.

We spoke in those weeks about the three finals that we had lost. We wanted to use that disappointment and that hurt. Do you remember it? Do you remember that feeling? Do you remember how devastating it was? We're only the managers, they would tell us. We can only give you so much. You are the ones on the pitch. You have to be the ones who do it. Don't come back in afterwards saying that we should have done this or we should have done that. Don't wait for another day. Do it today.

We wanted to do it for the management. We wanted to do it for ourselves. We wanted to do it for the county, for the supporters and for the jersey. And there was one other person we wanted to do it for. We wanted to do it for Paddy Phelan.

Paddy had given everything to Leitrim hurling. If there was a job, big or small, that needed to be done, Paddy would do it – particularly if it was a job that nobody else wanted to do. It was Paddy who had given me my first hurl that day back in Carrick.

'Don't mind the scoreboard,' he used to tell us. 'The scores will come.' He had seen so much hurling in his life. He had seen so many teams go a couple of points down, and then their heads would go completely. They let a tricky situation turn into a disaster because they didn't stay focused on the next score, the next ball. He had seen it happen with us as we let so many winnable games slip through our fingers.

Even when Paddy got sick, he would still be there at training sessions and still be at our games. It was obvious that he wasn't well but that never stopped him. He was a hundred per cent committed, the same as he ever was. He had been in the stands in Croke Park for the 2017 Lory Meagher final. He would never have missed that day, no matter what. He was so proud of us, so proud of what we had achieved, and he made sure that we knew it.

When Paddy died in February 2018, Leitrim hurling lost one of its great men. We had come so far, but we hadn't managed to win a national title while he was alive to celebrate it with us. We could do it now in his memory. We felt that would be the greatest tribute of all.

From the moment I woke up on the morning of the final,

my mind was on the game. Throw-in was at midday, and everything between now and then was its own little milestone, a signpost to say that we were getting closer and closer: what time we'd get out of bed, what time we'd meet for breakfast, what time the bus would collect us, what time we'd pull up on Jones' Road and see Croke Park waiting there to welcome us, inviting us to come in and make our history. I imagined myself out on the pitch. I tried to put myself in the moment and feel the energy that I would experience, our fans in the stands willing us on, the bodies moving all around me, our lads and theirs, closing off angles, calling for the ball, looking for space. When I got my chance, what pass would I pick? What option would I choose?

It was a beautiful June day. The conditions were perfect for an All-Ireland final and, I felt, perfect for a player like me. Even though I had only started one game in league and championship that season, I still thought I would be picked to play. I didn't know one way or the other until the morning of the final when the management read down through their list and got to the six starting forwards: Ben, Colm, Adam, Gavin, Clement and Cathal. I was on the bench, and so was Stephen. I was disappointed, but Michael had a word with the two of us and reminded us that our job started right now too. We would be needed. Be ready to go on.

We took the best of what Lancashire could throw at us in that first half and we held strong. At half time, we were three points up, 1-10 to 1-7. We were halfway there, and we might never have a better chance than this. The second half was an entirely different story though. For twenty long minutes, they ran the show, we were second best to everything, and the big scoreboards at either end of the stadium told that story. They scored seven points and we didn't manage a single one; we had gone from being four points up and in control to three points down and struggling. I was watching Michael on the sideline, waiting for his call. I was ready to go.

There was only twelve or thirteen minutes left. We needed a point, just one so that we could hang in there. Colm scored a beauty from the first row of the Hogan Stand, but Lancashire had us up against the wall and they weren't letting us go. They hit back with two quick points of their own. We were four behind, 1-17 to 1-13. The clock went past sixty minutes. I put on my helmet and came down to the sideline. Ben scored a point to bring us back within three again, and when the ball went dead, I was sent on.

The time for beautiful hurling had passed. The game became scrappy, frantic, a little bit desperate. When we came forward in possession, I tried to be clever, tried to find a gap here or there so that we could keep our width. If I got the ball in space, great. If not, I could help to keep things stretched and maybe make a yard for somebody else. We were still three points down at the end of the seventy minutes, and the referee signalled for an additional five.

I never panicked. We had five minutes to save ourselves, and I knew that we only needed one. That's the beauty of hurling. It's so fast, it only takes a split second for a chance to appear out of nothing. I'd played in so many games that had been turned on their head in a heartbeat. The clock ticked and ticked, and Lancashire got closer and closer to victory, but I never stopped believing.

Cathal put the ball on the end of his hurl and ran at Lancashire. He popped it to Clement. I was in space, screaming for the pass, but he was surrounded. I thought that he was fouled, that it would be a free in from the 21-yard line, dead centre, but there was no whistle. Clement saw me. He did well to get the ball away anyway but only as far as a Lancashire defender. I had to get to him, to put the clearance under pressure, and I did.

He only got it as far as the 45, where Ben scooped it up again. Cathal was all alone when the pass reached him. He moved it on to me. There was nobody near me. I had time for a shot, but I didn't have a great angle. It didn't matter – it was goals we needed now. I stepped back outside the defender as he raced in to tackle me and lifted my head. There were two or three green and gold jerseys in space, but none of them were in as good a position as James. He knew that we were running out of time, that any opportunity might be our last, and he gambled. He followed the ball up the field from his centre-back position and arrived on the edge of the D just as I picked my pass. James took the ball out of the air with his left hand and flashed it past the Lancashire keeper without breaking stride. There was the sound of ash on leather, and then the sound of the ball hitting the back of the net; the next sound was of the Leitrim fans going wild in the stand, making nearly enough noise to fill the entire ground. We were level.

The referee blew his whistle before either side had a chance to get one last shot away in search of a winner. It was all over, a draw, 2-16 to 1-19. But as we went back in to the dressing room to catch our breath and get set for extra time, I knew we had them. We knew they wouldn't be able to match us for fitness in an extra twenty minutes. Michael had made sure of it, lap after lap after lap, and now it was about to pay off when we needed it the most.

By the end of the first period of extra time, we were three up, and I had got my name on the scoresheet. The ball bobbled free out of a group of players and I got to it quickest to scoop it up. I was running away from the goal but I knew where the posts were and fired over a lovely point off my right. Every minute that went by took us a minute closer, and this time, we would make no mistake. When Clement was fouled for a penalty in the final minute of extra time, Gavin played it safe and tapped it over for a point rather than going for goal. It put us five ahead with time practically up, and even though Lancashire managed one last sting of their own with a point and then a goal, it was too little too late.

We didn't even have time to worry about it. As soon as Declan Molloy, our goalkeeper and captain, pucked the ball out, the referee blew the final whistle and the game was over. A wave of pure happiness washed across the Croke Park pitch and swept us all away. We were the 2019 Lory Meagher Cup champions. We had been wandering in the wilderness, but Martin had told us over and over again about this magical place, this promised land, and we had finally made it. The two of us hugged in the middle of the pitch. He had asked me to give him one year when I started out back in 2012. One year, that was all, and I said I would. Instead, he had given me eight years that I would never forget, a group of friends who were more like brothers to me than team-mates, and now this, the happiest day of my life. The road to Croke Park had taken us through so many twists and turns, but we had finally followed it all the way to our dream.

Our prize was waiting for us in the Hogan Stand. Declan climbed those famous steps and we piled up behind him. He closed his eyes, took a deep breath, and then did what every Leitrim hurler had wanted to do for a very long time. Thousands of hands lifted that trophy with him, every single player who had worn that green and gold jersey with such pride before us. They were the people who started the journey and who carried it on through some dark years; we were the lucky ones who got the opportunity to finish it on their behalf.

I didn't see my family until a little while later. When I came out of the stadium, they were waiting for me across the road, outside the Croke Park Hotel, my brothers still proudly wearing their Leitrim tops, and my mam beside them with the biggest smile on her face. She didn't need to tell me how much it meant to her. It wasn't just the happiest moment of my life; it was the happiest of hers since the day we had first arrived in our new home seventeen years earlier. I could only wish that my dad had been there with us to share this moment too. I know how proud he would have been.

The celebrations started in Ryan's that afternoon and went on for a week. Whether it was in Carrick, or Manorhamilton, or Ballinamore, we were joined by great GAA people, old and young, from all over Leitrim. The parties went on late into the night. Together, we had all waited a very long time for this day to come. Now that it was finally here, we had no intention of rushing it.

TO BE IRISH

My Irish citizenship means everything to me.
People might look at my life and presume
that my identity must be a complicated jigsaw,
but to me it is very simple and it has been for a long time:
I am Kurdish-Irish. I lived here for years without having
an Irish passport – without having any passport – but in
terms of my rights and security and protection from the
state, I never really felt any different from any of the other
Irish people I know. The day I received my citizenship, 27
July 2021, was a very proud moment. It made official what
I have known for a very long time: Ireland is where I live,
and it is also where I belong.

I was the last in my family to apply for citizenship, and
the last to get it. I didn't have any doubt about whether or
not I wanted to become an Irish citizen, but I was intimidated
by the amount of paperwork involved and the prospect

that, even if the whole process went well and as quickly as possible, it would take at least a year. In the end, a year would have been a great result.

No matter how equal I felt, there were little reminders over the years that I was different. Whenever I was interviewed for jobs, there were questions about visas and other documents to prove that I was legally allowed to work; if you're an Irish citizen, those questions don't exist. Being in Ireland was fine, for the most part, as long as I stayed here – but if I had been travelling abroad and I was trying to come back into the country, there were usually a few extra hoops to jump through.

There was the day when I was separated from the rest of my Leitrim team-mates at immigration in Dublin Airport. We were flying back home from England after a game against one of the Exiles, and I was steered away from everybody else and into a queue marked Non-EU. I know that's the system but I had lived in Ireland for fifteen years at that stage, and I was upset and annoyed that I was being singled out. I queued for nearly two hours before I was allowed to go through and go home; the worst part was that the rest of the squad waited outside for me that whole time. It was embarrassing.

In the grand scheme of things, they were little inconveniences, but I was fed up with being made to feel different. I got in touch with a solicitor to start my application, and I quickly remembered why I had been putting it off for so long. Everything was complicated.

'Have you got your birth cert?' the solicitor asked, working through the checklist one line at a time.

'I don't have a birth cert. I never had one.'

Instead, I had to send in an explanation that I had been, in effect, born in no man's land – but when the paperwork was submitted, that would be the first thing the system flagged: no birth cert supplied; application incomplete; back into the queue again.

There's no end to the documents you have to submit. I was sending payslips, proof of earnings, the whole lot. There was one occasion when my application was rejected because I was only working part-time. I had just got my job with Zoetis, the big pharmaceutical manufacturing multinational where I work now, but my start date had been pushed back by a couple of weeks and I was only doing bits and pieces of work while I waited. That was a red flag in the system even though I came here as a programme refugee, which means that I'm entitled to the same rights as any other Irish person in Ireland; it shouldn't have mattered how many hours I was working. I tried to make my case and explain that, but it didn't make the slightest bit of difference. My application was refused and I had to go all the way back to the start.

There were forms to fill in, and letters to write, and documents to photocopy and send, and eventually I got an application reference number to say that I was finally in the system. And then the back-and-forth started all over again:

'We need you to send us this document, please.'

'But I already sent that.'

'We need you to send it again, sorry.'

There was a time when my file went missing altogether – 'Sorry, we don't have your application' – even though I had my reference number and proof that it had been delivered by registered post. Someone looked around and found it for me eventually. And then, just when the finish line seemed to be in sight, Covid came to Ireland and shut down the entire country.

When all the paperwork was done and my day finally came in the summer of 2021 and I officially became an Irish citizen, it was so special to join more than a thousand others who were also receiving their citizenship that day. Covid meant that it had to be a virtual ceremony, and we couldn't all be there in person together, but fittingly for me, it was held in Croke Park. A day like that is a wonderful celebration of Irishness – in a traditional sense, but also in a very new and modern sense; we were the faces of a changing country that had welcomed us in as one of their own.

It was an honour to be asked to share my story on the day as a representative of Ireland's newest citizens. It was a privilege to hold a passport for the first time in my life, and I couldn't have been more proud that it was an Irish one. As a Kurd, and as a refugee, I never had my own country until that day. I will always have my heritage, but Ireland is my home.

The road to becoming a citizen was a long one for me – nineteen years, two counties, and one All-Ireland medal in the making, if we're counting – but you don't become Irish just because a piece of paper says so. Being Irish is not about where you were born or how you look. It is about who you are and how you feel. The reality is that I have been Irish for a long, long time. For that, I can never thank Ireland enough.

EPILOGUE

Every job I've had, so many of the opportunities and doors that have been opened for me, have all been because of the GAA. It has given me so many of my friends, great people who will be in my life for ever, and so many happy days. It has given me a community that I love and where I know that I belong. It has given me a place to call home.

Coming to Ireland from Al-Tash camp was like walking into a gold mine. We say that when you die, you go to heaven – but in Ireland, I felt that I was already in heaven. In 2019, I was able to buy an apartment in Dublin. Having my own front door, my own keys, my own space was a luxury that I never dared to imagine when I was growing up in a mud house in a refugee camp. No life is perfect. No country is perfect. But even when times are at their toughest here in Ireland, I still feel that I am exceptionally lucky.

My apartment is in Tallaght; I can't think of anywhere else that I would rather live. You never know where the ups and downs of life will take you, but it's hard to see myself ever leaving here. And for as long as I am in Tallaght, I will be in Thomas Davis.

The club is a part of who I am. It's how I see myself, and how other people see me. You can't separate the two: I am a Thomas Davis man. I'm always there; my life is my home, my work and my club, and I wouldn't have it any other way. I feel like it is *my* club, like I own it – and everybody else who is involved has that same feeling. That's why I care about it so much. That's what makes it such a special place.

I love the club's history, which goes all the way back to 1888. If you go up to a match, or a training session, or the clubhouse, you'll meet people who played in the club years ago, and they're still involved because their kids or grandkids are playing now. I have already started to get my nephews and nieces involved. The heart of the club gets passed along from generation to generation; that's what keeps it alive.

It doesn't matter which of our teams are playing, whether it's the senior hurlers or the Division 10 footballers – I always want us to win. I always want Thomas Davis to keep developing, to keep improving, to be at the highest level we can be and represent our community proudly while we're doing it. Winning the intermediate championship in 2017 was a massive moment for us as a club, but for me personally, it was even more special in 2019 to be promoted to the Senior A hurling championship for the first time in our history. There were no trophies and no medals that day because we lost out to Scoil Uí Chonaill in the Senior B final, but bringing the club all the way through the grades, one win at a time, until we were right at the top had always been our ambition. Very few people outside the club would ever have expected us to make it that far – we're still seen as a 'football club' sometimes – and even though we were relegated again in 2021, we proved to everyone, and ourselves, that we could belong there.

There's no doubt that the club was a massive help in how I integrated into Irish society. It wasn't just that it introduced me to one or two lads I made friends with, it was the whole team, the whole club. If I want to go up there on a Saturday evening, I don't need to ring ahead to see if anyone's around to join me. I can sit there with anybody, and talk to anybody, because everybody knows each other. The more time I spent in the club, the more I understood about the things that make Ireland so unique: the history, the culture, the slagging and the craic, the couple of pints, but more than anything, the people.

After winning the Lory Meagher with Leitrim in 2019, I played on for one more year and then retired from inter-county hurling. There was no more silverware, unfortunately – we were beaten by Sligo in the Division 3B league final and then lost out to Mayo in the semi-finals of the Nicky

Rackard Cup. I wasn't sure if it was the right time for me to go, whether or not I had another year left to give, but the 2020 season was disrupted by Covid, and as it got into the winter and games were finally being played, the writing was on the wall. I was about to turn thirty, and I wasn't getting any younger. I was busier in work, still trying to juggle club and county and fit it all in around twelve-hour shifts. I could see my performances starting to suffer and in the end, something had to give. Walking away from that Leitrim dressing room was an incredibly difficult thing to do, but I could do it with no regrets. Our dreams had already come true. We would always have Croke Park on 22 June 2019.

I can't imagine my life without the GAA. I love that I am able to give a little back by coaching the kids' teams in Thomas Davis. Every year, I promise myself that I will take a break and step back for a year, but I never do; I'd miss it too much. Ireland is changing, becoming more multicultural and diverse by the day, and the best thing the GAA can do is make sure that their coaches, their games promotion officers, anyone who has a stake in the future of the sport, reflect that. The kids who are in school now are going to be the stars in ten or fifteen years' time. These kids need to see coaches and ambassadors who look like they do, who can encourage them to get involved and stay involved in the GAA. They need to see stars from all different backgrounds so that they can follow in their footsteps. The GAA changed my life and I will never forget that. There are tens of thousands more young kids just like me who are coming up behind me; it can change theirs too.

I will for ever be grateful to Ireland, to its people, for the gift it has given me and my family. Nobody ever wants to be a refugee. It's not something you choose. You do it because it is the only way to survive. Life can change in an instant when war comes to your doorstep, like it did for my family in 1980, but the basic truths of life never change. We are all human beings. We all want the same things: to grow up, to have somewhere to go home to at night, to have family and friends and to be safe. We have all come from somewhere, and we are all going somewhere too. We might look different but our blood is the same.

Every single person in this world has a story. This is mine.

ACKNOWLEDGEMENTS

To individually thank everybody who has helped me and my family since we first arrived in Ireland more than twenty years ago would take another book. Only some of them are named here, but to all of those people, know how much I appreciate everything that you've done for us; I cannot thank you enough.

Thank you to all of my schoolteachers, both at St Mary's National School in Carrick and at Old Bawn Community School in Tallaght. A special thanks to Michael Keane in Old Bawn for all of his help over the years.

Thank you to the people of Leitrim. Thanks to everybody at both St Mary's GAA club in Carrick-on-Shannon and at Carrick Hurling Club, where my GAA career first started, and to everybody in Leitrim GAA. Thank you to Barry Singleton and the Singleton family, Fintan Cox, Cormac Flynn, Kevin Kennedy, Anthony Conway, Martin Cunniffe and the Cunniffe family, Paddy O'Connor, and the late Paddy Phelan. May he rest in peace.

Thanks also to all of those wonderful people who helped me and my family to settle into our new lives during our first days in Carrick-on-Shannon: to Martina Glennon from the Department of Justice as well as to Tom Finnerty, Paul Hamilton, Vincent Gilligan, and Christine McGowan.

Thank you to the people of Tallaght, and to the people of Thomas Davis GAA. Thank you to Shane Plowman; Corky – Denis O'Donovan – my hurling manager at juvenile level; Mary Hoey, who invites me to the house for Christmas every year; Terry Carthy and the Carthy family; Mick Kirby and the Kirby family; Pat Courtney; Mick Byrne and the Byrne family; and Paul and David Nugent from Kingsbury Furniture in Tallaght.

Thank you to all of those businesses and individuals who have sponsored and supported the club and county in various ways. Thank you to The Bush Hotel, PJ Clarke's New York, Derek Tyrrell and Tyrrellair, Declan Ryan, Azad Shirazi of Zaytoon, and Ryan's of Camden Street for their support of Leitrim GAA and Leitrim hurling. Thank you to our club sponsors at Thomas Davis, including O'Connor Heating and Plumbing, Airways Canopy and Duct Cleaning Services, Peadar Browns of Clanbrassil Street, and Baxto Kebab in Tallaght. Thanks also to Westpark Fitness and ROS Nutrition for supporting me.

ACKNOWLEDGEMENTS

Thank you to all of the team at Gill Books who worked so hard to make this book a reality. Thank you to Seán Hayes, who first approached me with the idea, and to Aoibheann Molumby, Rachael Kilduff, Laura King, Fiona Murphy, Charlie Lawlor, and everybody else involved in producing this book. Thank you to Niall Kelly, who helped me to tell my story. Thanks also to Prof. Barzoo Eliassi and Dr Dilman Ahmed for their advice.

Finally, to my family and extended family, in Ireland, Kurdistan, and around the world: thank you all.